BATTLEFIEL

KENT AND
SUSSEX 1940

BRITAIN'S FRONT LINE

Air raid practice (see p. 130).

KENT AND SUSSEX 1940

BRITAIN'S FRONT LINE

STUART HYLTON

Pen & Sword
MILITARY

To Leigh and Pat Herington
my good friends and genial hosts during the research for this book

First published in Great Britain in 2004 by
PEN & SWORD MILITARY
an imprint of
Pen & Sword Books Limited
47 Church Street
Barnsley
South Yorkshire
S70 2AS

Copyright © Stuart Hylton, 2004

ISBN: 1 84415 084 4

The right of Stuart Hylton to be identified as Author
of this Work has been asserted by him in accordance
with the Copyright, Designs and Patents Act 1988.

A CIP catalogue record for this book
is available from the British Library

Typeset in 9pt Palatino by Pen & Sword Books Limited

Printed and bound in England by
CPI UK

Pen & Sword Books Ltd incorporates the imprints of
Pen & Sword Aviation, Pen & Sword Maritime, Pen & Sword Military,
Wharncliffe Local History, Pen & Sword Select,
Pen & Sword Military Classics and Leo Cooper

For a complete list of Pen & Sword titles please contact:
PEN & SWORD BOOKS LIMITED
47 Church Street, Barnsley, South Yorkshire, S70 2AS, England
email: enquiries@pen-and-sword.co.uk • website: www.pen-and-sword.co.uk

Contents

Assembling an Anderson air raid shelter – a familiar process during the early months of the war.

Rescue workers practise evacuating an air raid casualty.

Introduction
and Acknowledgements

Some local history is much more than local in its significance. A couple of years ago, when I wrote a history of the city of Manchester, I soon came to realise that the local events I was describing were ones that set a course for the nation and, in some cases, the whole British Empire, over a century or more. Something similar is true of the events that took place in, around and over Kent and Sussex in 1940. Had those events taken a different turn, the subsequent story of Europe and the entire free world could have been very different.

In 1940, Kent and Sussex were at the centre of the world's attention. The apparently invincible Nazi war machine had swept across continental Europe, and most of the world – including most people in Britain and Germany – expected southern England to be the next to face the onslaught. As we now know, Kent and Sussex would have borne the brunt of that invasion, had it come.

Following the evacuation from Dunkirk, the British authorities attempted to rebuild their shattered armed forces and to prepare the south-east corner of the country as a battlefield. As they were doing so, the Germans began to devote the vast resources of the Reich to their invasion plans. If, as some suggest, it was all a bluff, there was never such a gigantic and elaborate bluff in all the history of warfare. At the same time, the tens of thousands of people living in Kent and Sussex were struggling to continue something resembling a normal life in their communities.

What I have tried to do in this book is to take a slice through a piece of history, looking both at the leading world players and their grand strategies and at the attempts of ordinary people to make sense of the extraordinary events through which they were living. It is not intended to be a conventional account of the events of the war. I have tried to give that big picture in just enough detail to make sense of what was happening in the local community, but no more.

Equally, I have not tried to do the job of a conventional local history, in terms for example of detailing who was bombed when, or to give the story of individual Home Guard units. Kent and Sussex are very fortunate in the rich variety of their coverage by local historians. There are many good books that will provide far more local detail than there is space for in my volume, and many of these are listed in my bibliography. I hope that my efforts will encourage those of you who are not familiar with them to investigate them further. If I achieve anything through this book, I hope it is to give a flavour of what it was like to live through these times. Often it is the minutiae of life that best give this flavour, as people try to adapt everyday life to fit around the sweep of world events.

Then, as now, local newspapers laid a fascinating finger on the pulse of the local community. I have drawn heavily upon them, both for the local stories they tell and for the advertisements that bring the period so vividly to life. The Second World War photographs, with one exception, are reproduced by the kind permission of the *Kent Messenger* Group of newspapers from their splendid collection. I am grateful to Simon Irwin and his colleagues for their help in this. Some of the wartime railway scenes in the *Messenger* collection were originally photographed by the Southern Railway Company. The frontispiece of the railway gun being fired came from Dover Library, part of Kent County Council. I have tried to track down the copyright holders for all the images used in the book, in one or two cases without success, but have tried to ensure that these are at least duly acknowledged. If there are any failings in this respect and the copyright holders would care to draw them to my attention via the publisher, I will try to ensure that they are remedied in any future edition.

Chapter One

'Tonbridge is largely normal'

(a headline in the *Kent and Sussex Courier*, 1 September 1939)

Yesterday everyone went quietly about their business without any dread of possible alarm... Everywhere one came across optimistic people displaying a calm characteristic of the Britisher. Kent and Sussex Courier, 25 August 1939

The summer of 1939 was drawing to a close. August turned to September and, on the face of it, the tranquil pattern of English life was continuing uninterrupted. The holiday season was in full swing and the seaside resorts were packed with people enjoying the sunshine. Business, hit by bad weather in the early summer, was at last booming:

Outfitters, who have perhaps been the hardest hit of all tradesmen, are now doing a splendid trade in light summer dresses, bathing costumes and sportswear... If the weather continues to hold good for several weeks, we expect to recover from the effects of the trade depression. Kent Messenger, 26 August 1939

The Mayor of Ramsgate was full of confidence for the future:

On our shores today you could not find a happier crowd... I feel that in a year or two Ramsgate will be the leading resort of the country. Kent Messenger, 26 August 1939

Messrs P and A Campbell were offering pleasure sailings from the piers at Brighton and Hastings (weather and circumstances permitting). The Southern Railway was running 'Cheap trips to the Continent from Folkestone and Dover: Boulogne from 10 shillings. Passports are not required by British subjects.' For the more adventurous traveller, the Continental Express Company could provide excursions to a range of continental locations, including Germany. Going to the extremes of adventurousness, two men arrived in Kent with an 18-foot collapsible canoe, announcing their intention to paddle to Australia. The next week they were planning to cross to France, making their way to the Mediterranean via the inland waterways of continental Europe. It was a bad week to start out. They got as far as Sheerness before their canoe drifted away from them and they had to be taken to Leigh-on-Sea to retrieve it.

At home, Alan Russell and his *Laughter Unlimited* show at the Hastings Pier Theatre was sending the audiences home with aching ribs. This 'sparkling and happy programme' featured Charlie, the popular naughty boy of the show. 'His clever fooling never fails to reduce one to almost helpless laughter,' the *Hastings Observer* promised. The cinemas were showing Shirley Temple in *The Little Princess*. 'The laughter, the tears, the drama, the tenderness of this great story are impressively presented,' the *Sussex Daily News* told its readers. In Folkestone, the entertainment was live, as the town prepared to welcome Bertram Mills's Circus,

An example of wartime humour – has our taste in matters comic changed so dramatically since the 1940s?

whose big top held 4,000 people and was the largest in Britain. 'Some idea of the magnitude of the show may be gathered by the fact that three special trains are used to convey the circus and menagerie from town to town,' said the Dover Express and East Kent News. It was due to open on 4 September. Live entertainment was also on offer at the Royal Hippodrome, Chatham, where the Gordon Ray Young Ladies promised 'a treat for the tired businessman'. Those not wishing to be over-excited might have preferred the Linton Women's Institute, where 'Miss Anderson gave a very interesting talk on "The comfort of the feet", with several useful hints on corns and rheumatism.' Employers were still advertising for staff. A 'smart intelligent boy' was wanted as a chocolate seller (salary 10 shillings – 50p today – a week, plus commission). At the more genteel end of the jobs market a 'gentlewoman of mature years (over forty) desirous of augmenting income, is offered congenial employment with permanent income.' If you were neither smart, intelligent nor genteel, there was always 'Lad wanted; able to ride cycle. Early riser and willing' or 'Wanted: strong girl as general.' (This latter was a general domestic servant, not fast-track promotion in the armed forces). Those wanting a military career could join the Royal Air Force:

> *Learn a trade in the RAF. Vacancies for unskilled men of good education to train as wireless operators, armourers and instrument repairers... All jobs well paid and with liberal annual leave.*

Journeys to work in Brighton would have to be made without the aid of the town's trams, which were being replaced by trolley buses and something called 'heavy-oil-engine buses'. Enthusiasts could buy their very own Brighton tram for the bargain price of £5 (buyer collects, and you could not use the Corporation's tram tracks to get it home).

Small boys were doing what small boys have done since time immemorial. Three of them were summoned to appear at Hastings Police Court, where they were fined 5 shillings apiece for damaging the wall of the Borough Sanatorium in the process of scrumping apples.

At the county cricket ground in Hove, Sussex were being trounced by the champions, Yorkshire. Hutton and Yardley scored centuries for the visitors and Verity took 7 for 9 as Sussex were skittled out for 33 in their second innings. But Sussex supporters seeking solace in the tea tent would have noticed that something was amiss:

> The order for the evacuation of London children and their reception at Brighton, Hove and elsewhere robbed the tea tent on the county cricket ground at Hove yesterday of a good number of its working personnel...
>
> Over 30% of the waitresses in all sections were unable to help owing to the prior demand of 'voluntary service' and one section, run by Lady Wishart and presided over yesterday by her daughter, Mrs Tessier, was deprived of every one of its personnel for this reason. Sussex Daily News, 1 September 1939

Germany had invaded Poland and war was days away. The British authorities were carrying out plans to evacuate some 3.5 million civilians (mostly women and children) from the major cities and other danger areas to what were designated 'safe areas'. Extraordinarily, as it now seems, the coastal towns directly facing continental Europe were considered safe and preparations were made for them to receive thousands of evacuees from London. At the same time, children living along the Thames Estuary were themselves to be evacuated. Some of the children from Chatham, Rochester, Gillingham, Northfleet and Gravesend were being taken by pleasure steamer to ports in Suffolk and Norfolk and distributed inland from there. Others would go by train to destinations unknown. Parents were told to write their child's name on a strong piece of paper and sew it into their clothes. The authorities promised 'every child will be labelled and will carry a postcard to send home on arrival at their evacuation places.' With them went their schoolteachers and, for the younger children, their mothers, thereby creating some of the first tragic victims of the war. The *Kent Messenger* christened these 'the washupees'. They were the helpless (some would say hopeless) husbands who suddenly found themselves deprived of their wife's domestic ministrations. The paper reported that:

> In the Medway towns there are crowds of grass widowers who are piling up unwashed crocks and bundles of soiled linen, relying with pathetic faith on tin openers and realising as never before what jewels of wives they had. A Chatham man spoke for them all. 'When you have been used to relying on a woman, you're lost when she goes away. There are 75 per cent of us in the same position around here.' Kent Messenger, 16 September 1939

He was down to his last two clean shirts and the privations of wartime were already starting to look overwhelming. Everywhere, there were the first small signs of the dramatic changes that were to overtake the people of Kent and Sussex. The Mayor of Dover was advising his citizens that the number of street lamps was to be reduced and arrangements made for the rest to be extinguished at short notice. He also recommended that householders should acquire a store of non-perishable foods. (The storing of more than a week's supply of food would later cease to be prudent housekeeping and would become hoarding, an offence under the Defence of the Realm Regulations punishable by a fine and confiscation). After appealing for volunteers to form Rescue, Repair and Decontamination Squads, and giving out the locations of air-raid shelters, the Mayor continued: 'I appeal to everyone to remain calm. The Council and their officers have everything well in hand and are prepared for any emergency.'

But business knew better. Large advertisements for Aspro advised: 'Don't let these trying times upset you. You can depend on Aspro to calm your nerves.' Products as diverse as Guinness and Wrigley's chewing gum advertised their soothing qualities in a crisis:

During the early stages of the war, schoolchildren would often wear their gas masks in class for a few minutes each day, as a means of acclimatisation.

Wrigley's chewing gum 'steadies your nerves.' In times of stress, Wrigley's gum quiets your nerves, soothes your throat and keeps you mentally alert. It also aids digestion, apt to be impaired under strain.

Other businesses were quick to seize new commercial opportunities. Ironmongers started to turn out incendiary-bomb scoops and rakes (7s 6d the pair) or paraffin stoves for your air-raid shelter (15s 9d). Tapley's Motors would equip your car with headlamp shields and all the other modifications needed to comply with the new Motor Car Lighting Regulations. Brooker's the opticians could supply special gas-mask sides for your spectacles. Builders offered to gas-proof any room in your house, and for the status-obsessed, there was even the opportunity to go one-up on your neighbours by having Overington's (**the** concrete specialists) build you a bespoke air-raid shelter to your own specifications. But the ultimate in status was surely the Bruce air-raid shelter. After the war, you could simply remove its roof and use it as a swimming pool. The *Kent Messenger* even ran an advertising feature for all these new domestic essentials. Those traders with no new wartime lines to sell simply appealed to the patriotic instinct for panic-buying:

Keep the flag flying!... *The life of the nation must go on. During the war 1914-18 many goods were practically unobtainable and prices soared to quite three times the price we are offering our goods today. We strongly advise you to come and buy TODAY... Supplies of many articles have already been entirely cut off in order to supply the forces.*

But for some shoppers, the outbreak of war meant business absolutely as usual. When retailers responded to losses of staff and shortages of petrol by reducing the frequency of their deliveries, there were howls of complaint in some quarters, with threats to take their custom elsewhere if delivery on demand were not restored. One Hastings woman insisted upon the immediate delivery of a single small cake of soap that would have fitted inside her handbag. Their threats were futile, since the new delivery arrangements had been agreed between all the local traders. By 1942 it would get even worse. Petrol shortages meant housewives living within a mile of the shopping centre were asked to adopt a 'cash and carry' system, whilst deliveries to addresses outside this radius were limited to once a week.

Even more unpopular was the Government's (short-lived) panic measure of closing cinemas and other places of entertainment at the outbreak of war. The Hastings Town Council Emergency Committee protested that the Government did not appreciate the seriousness of what it was doing. Experienced staff were being laid off, and would be difficult to replace. Other venues, equally likely to attract a large crowd (such as churches or shops) were not being treated the same way. Moreover, it would drive people into the arms of the publicans.

On the subject of the demon drink, the outbreak of hostilities also seemed to give new impetus to anyone with a bee in their bonnet. Teetotallers used the war as an excuse to redouble their efforts to bring in prohibition. A Mr Walter Mayo gave a talk to the Protestant Reformation Society, explaining that this war had been

FREE CAR PARK **REGENT** **DOVER** **TELEPHONE 747**

SUNDAY, JAN. 21st—One Day Only— Continuous from 3.0 p.m.
Florence Rice & Una Merkel in ALSO Mickey Rooney & Wallace Beery in
"FOUR GIRLS IN WHITE" (U) "STABLEMATES" (U)

Monday, Jan. 22nd (for Six Days) Continuous from 2.0 p.m.
Doors open 1.30 p.m.
Regent proudly presents a miracle of Screen Dramatisation

THE LION HAS WINGS
AN EPIC OF THE R.A.F.
MERLE OBERON - RALPH RICHARDSON
Produced by Alexander Korda
Daily at 3.31, 6.24 & 9.17.
—— ALSO ——

THE RUDD FAMILY GOES TO TOWN
Daily at 2.0, 4.53 & 7.46 p.m. with BERT BAILEY (U)

Monday, January 29th, for 3 days only—
"A GIRL MUST LIVE" & "MR. MOTO ON DANGER ISLAND"

'The Lion has Wings' was an early example of a wartime propaganda film, made with the active support of the Ministry of Information (who took a cut of the profits in return for their help).

started to defend a Catholic nation (Poland), just as the last one had (in that case, Belgium). Mr Mayo warmed to his subject, his argument starting to have some alarming echoes of Hitler's intolerance towards the Jews:

> We are now faced with two aggressions, the Germanic and the Papal, and we were at war to resist both in the defence of liberty and freedom... Our Protestant country is the champion of liberty, but the Roman aggression opposed freedom as regards worship and civil rights... The Bible proves the Roman Catholic Church is anti-Christian. Hastings and St Leonards Observer, 21 October 1939

Others accused the churches generally of what they saw as the crime of pacifism. One correspondent, calling himself for some reason 'Britain for the British' complained:

> The public have a right to know who are the clerics who have permitted church property under their control to be used for holding conscience-training classes and mock tribunals to teach the Conscientious Objectors the best sort of lies to tell the tribunals. The use of church halls was most improper... Pacifism is a throwback to the frightful excesses of religious mania which followed, but were not a result of, the reformation. Hastings and St Leonards Observer, 2 September 1939

He went on to claim that pacifism was a result of literal compliance with individual religious texts which, in another context, had given us the Adamites, who 'practised what is now called nudism.'

Amid these fears of naked pacifists running amok (in a peaceful sort of way) there were also those who sympathised directly with the Fascist ideology. In Capel-le-Ferne, just outside Dover, anti-semitic posters were put up overnight, apparently directed at those who had given shelter to some of the Jewish refugees arriving from Europe. They called on the authorities to 'Conscript the Jews. It's their war! Let them fight it, not finance it.' The war memorial in the Butter Market, Canterbury had anti-war slogans and Fascist symbols painted on it.

Life took on a darker side in other ways. In St John's Parish Hall, Hollington, the usual demonstrations of rug-making or fruit-bottling were replaced by 'How to protect your baby from poison gas,' and someone calling themselves 'A lover of animals' was calling on the public to have their pets put down now, rather than leave them to a fate of homelessness and starvation when the inevitable apocalypse came. Animal welfare was much on people's minds in these early days of the war. During the first air-raid alarm in Ramsgate, a woman rang the local police station to ask what she should do about her parrot. The officer's reply was not deemed printable by the local press. One householder allowed not only the milkman, but also his horse, to share her shelter during an alarm and a family in Herne Bay painted white stripes on their black cat, to make it more visible during the blackout. One lady, going against the trends, was actually advised to buy a pet. She applied for a petrol ration for her motor mower, and was told to get a goat instead.

Some 3,000 victims of Hitler's terror were living at the Kitchener Camp at Richborough, near Sandwich. Its occupants had turned it from a derelict relic of the First World War into a comfortable and lively township, with its own orchestra, band, cinema and other entertainments. The residents (men and youths only) supplemented their working day with compulsory English lessons, and received no pay, other than 6d (2½p) a week pocket money. They required a pass to leave the camp. The £80,000-a-year running costs of the camp were met largely by the Central Fund of British Jewry, though this was supplemented by an open day of entertainments (all in English) put on by the many artists and musicians among the camp's population. When war broke out, most of them volunteered for national service, and they went on to form five companies of the Royal Pioneer Corps, serving in France from early 1940.

Within days, the people of Sussex and Kent would find their lives beginning to change in a hundred other ways, small and large. Even before war broke out, *The Queen of the Channel*, a pleasure steamer out of Ramsgate and Margate, was refused permission to dock at Boulogne and turned around while still 6 miles out. All pleasure trips from the piers were soon cancelled and the fleets retreated to the relative safety of their home ports. Some of the steamers familiar to pleasure-trippers were commissioned as minesweepers. They and others would make the journey (for a good number, their final voyage) to Dunkirk the following year. The piers along the south coast were wired with explosives and had whole sections

The women and children of Gravesend prepare for war by digging air-raid trenches.

removed from them, to prevent them being used as landing points for invaders. The BBC was reduced to broadcasting a single programme, on new wavelengths, to prevent the Germans jamming them or using their stations as direction-finders for bombers. This new programme included frequent news broadcasts, (regardless of the fact that there was no news to broadcast) and even more incessant organ recitals by Sandy McPherson. Chief Constables called for all enemy aliens to register with the authorities; from now, their lives would be seriously curtailed and most would eventually lose their liberty. Others benefited from the crisis; lorry drivers attending Oxted Magistrates' Court, expecting to lose their licences for motoring offences, learned that it was 'in the national interest' that they should keep them.

Official instruction and information was in plentiful supply. People were told where the public shelters, emergency fire stations and first-aid posts were located (parents whose children had any of a range of infectious diseases were told to keep out of them); how to secure their homes against bombing and what to do if they were caught out in the street during an air raid. There were new sounds to listen out for – the rising and falling siren that warned of an air raid and the steady note that said the danger had passed; the football rattles that warned of gas, and the handbell that told them that the area was now clear.

There was the inevitable confusion at first. One woman motorist in Hastings, stopped by an air-raid warden to be told that there was an air raid and that she should take cover, thought her car was being commandeered. She leapt out, leaving the car unlocked and the engine running, and ran off to find a bus to get her home. A fire alarm going off at West Malling at 4.00 am one morning had hundreds of people running for the shelters and led to an unexpected call-out for the local Air Raid Precaution (ARP) staff.

There were calls for volunteers to fill sandbags to protect Brighton's hospitals ('bring your own implements if possible') and others volunteered their services without even being asked. In Lewes, sandbags were placed over the cellar lights on the pavement in the High Street but, it was proudly and improbably boasted, 'the work did not attract undue attention.' At various places across the town, 42-foot-long trenches accommodating fifty people were being planned for those who found themselves in the street during an air raid.

People queued for two hours or more to use public telephone boxes and waited in line at the Post Offices to send telegrams. There were runs on tinned food and blackout material in the shops, taxis were virtually unobtainable, but at least the beaches were not crowded. The effects on social life were random. North Brighton

Queuing – for almost everything – became one of the banes of wartime life.

Allotment Holders' Protection Society cancelled their annual show, and the joint expedition of the Worthing and Hove Archaeological Societies to Highdown Hill was also called off, but the Aquarium Restaurant in Brighton still shook to the exotic rhythms of Harold Simpson's Band and the dancing feet of the Brighton Telephone Area General and Sports Association (featuring Mr P Allcorn as MC). In Ramsgate, one dancehall banned long skirts, lest they caused people to trip during a dash to the shelters.

The call-up of the armed forces led to a rush on weddings. The Registrar's office at Ramsgate reported a threefold increase. Some had to be held so early in the morning that guests travelling any distance could not get there in time. Honeymoon plans were curtailed – in one case a man getting married had just one hour's leave, which must have put paid to even the most modest of honeymoon plans. One couple planned a military guard of honour, only to find that their guards had been called to more pressing duties. Later, once the initial panic (and flood of weddings) had subsided a little, members of the armed forces were normally allowed four days' leave to get married – so-called 'passionate leave'.

At Canterbury, air-raid precautions related to the cathedral became hugely controversial. First, Green Court, which had lain undisturbed for centuries, was dug up to provide air-raid trenches. The stained glass and other valuables were removed for safe-keeping and even the gilt weather vanes on Bell Harry Tower were removed, as being too visible at night. Most controversial of all, they decided to make the crypt a secure air-raid shelter for over a thousand people. This involved covering the floor of the choir and ambulatory of the cathedral with several feet of earth. Horses and carts and even a railway line into the cathedral were used to import the earth, putting much of the cathedral out of use for worship. Critics described the decision as 'desecration'.

Evacuees

But it was the evacuees that wrought the most dramatic changes to the communities of Kent and Sussex. Normal bus and train schedules were abandoned as plans were made get the children out of London and into their new billets. Each area had had its allocations worked out in detail. Bognor and District was promised some 6,000 over three days. There were plans to take over empty houses if enough voluntary billets could not be found. Chichester was to get 4,000 and its adjoining rural areas a further 9,000. Lewes and Chailey were promised a very precise 6,399, though the offers of voluntary billets had been disappointingly few and the organisers were having to wave the stick of compulsion at reluctant householders. Hove and Portslade's quota was 15,000, and they had use of the Lido Cinema Café as a relief centre. At least the children of the area had something to celebrate – pupils in Brighton were given an extended summer holiday, when schools were kept closed while arrangements for the new influx were made. Almost before the first evacuee had landed in Rustington, Mr William de Bellroche was organising classes in sketching and drawing for them up at the Manor House. Hastings was promised almost 3,000 child evacuees on 1 September. Other

Evacuees from St Michael's School in Chatham await their departure for 'somewhere in England'.

allocations included 7,434 to Sevenoaks and adjoining rural areas; 8,500 to Maidstone and its rural hinterland; Malling (7,000); Hollingbourne (4,000); Canterbury and its surrounding rural areas (4,560).

Brighton was said to be the biggest reception area for evacuees in the country, receiving a total of 30,000 'little guests', as the headlines referred to them. An appeal was launched there for high chairs and perambulators for the new arrivals. The Girl Guides of east Kent co-ordinated an appeal for cast-off clothing for the 'really poor and grateful people of Millwall, whose children are now evacuees in the county' and the Sussex WVS were looking for wool and blankets.

The newspapers warned that some of the evacuee children 'were bound to be more than a little high-spirited.' One couple found out what this meant when they left their children playing with the 'nice quiet boy from Limehouse' who had been billeted on them. They returned to find that he had stolen all their toys and was beating them over the head with the coal shovel. The evacuees' hosts, aided by the local press, exacted a form of revenge by laughing at their new guests' innocence of life outside of the impoverished inner city backgrounds from which so many of them came. Entire newspaper columns were given over to evacuees who thought that potatoes grew from trees like fruit, or that a cow was 'an 'orse wiv 'orns'. One child, seeing a chicken being plucked, enquired whether you had to undress the chickens every night, and another told her mother to bring her gas mask when visiting, since the pigs smelled. The Ministry of Information even promoted a competition to find the funniest howlers.

We were told of those who would not sleep in beds, for fear of falling out; who wondered where the holes in the bedroom walls were to let in the mice; who marvelled at a table setting with 'the same pattern on all the blinkin' cups' and who enquired whether they needed to remove their shoes before using the first full-sized bath they had ever seen. One even found the quiet uncanny: 'Mum and Dad always 'ave a row on Saturdays.'

A more serious cause of concern was that many people found it impossible to keep these hungry children on the 8s 6d a week that the Government paid for them. There were calls for the evacuees' parents to be made to contribute directly to their upkeep.

The evacuees also included people who were sick or disabled. The Royal Sussex Hospital sent its less urgent cases home and reopened two closed wards, in order to receive some 400 evacuated hospital cases. In addition:

During the weekend, it is expected that a hundred expectant mothers, three hundred blind people and a large number of crippled children will arrive from the London area. Hastings and St Leonards Observer, 2 September 1939

This led gossip-mongers to complain variously that local cases were being ignored in favour of the evacuees, and also that the evacuees' needs were themselves being inadequately treated.

For some, the additional pressure of war proved too much: John Drummond was a 45-year-old former schoolmaster who was recovering from a nervous breakdown. Shortly after he was told that he was to have five people billeted on him, he was found dead, with his head in the gas oven. A Brighton waiter, Frederick Cozens, collapsed and died during an air-raid practice on the day war broke out. The Coroner thought that the brain haemorrhage that killed him was brought on by the stress of the air-raid drill. A Benenden woman shot first her twelve-year-old daughter and then herself, and a woman from Tonbridge drowned herself. In both cases, war worries were cited by the Coroner as a major factor in the deaths.

The blackout

The blackout came into operation from the very start of the war: it was felt necessary at first to remind people that it was not optional. Within days, the first of many reports of road-traffic fatalities was reported – a Petham man walking the few yards between his home and his local was knocked down. Kent reported a 73 per cent increase in traffic accidents in September 1939, compared with the previous September. One of these involved the Regional Commissioner, Sir Auckland Geddes, who was run down by a lady cyclist while inspecting ARP measures in Hastings. In port towns, falling into the docks in the blackout was an additional hazard, and there were frequent reports of the lucky ones, who were pulled out alive, and the less fortunate. The really unfortunate might drown in the air-raid trenches; the one in Pencester Gardens, Dover, kept filling with water. It had been dug on the site of an underground spring.

The blackout soon began to be enforced in earnest and, unlike in some parts of England, public opinion in this area seemed to be quite militantly behind their enforcement:

LOOK OUT IN THE BLACKOUT

NEARLY 1,200 KILLED IN DECEMBER ALONE

Don't think that accidents only happen to other people. Tonight on your way home there will be danger. Don't step off the kerb without looking both ways. Throw the light of your torch down on the ground so that you do not dazzle drivers. You cannot risk taking any chances.

The blackout led to a dramatic increase in accidents. Even the Regional Commissioner was not immune.

> *Crowds gathered round the windows of a tailor's shop in a main thoroughfare in Brighton yesterday evening, where a light had been left on. The light shone brightly across the road and was reflected in the window of a shop on the opposite side. Eventually the manager of the shop arrived in a police car, and the light was switched off.* Sussex Daily News, 5 September 1939

Public opinion could get quite inflamed against anyone suspected of aiding and abetting the enemy. In Tunbridge Wells, a hostile crowd threatened to wreck a shop whose owner had failed to turn the lights off. A man in Ramsgate who failed to observe the blackout was fined £15: 'It was stated that a crowd of about forty people threatened to smash the windows and do injury to the defendant.' In Dover, a drunken shop manager pretended that he had sent a Morse-code message to a mysterious individual occupying a hotel room overlooking the sea. He had to be arrested for his own protection from an angry mob. Notwithstanding this groundswell of opinion, the local papers were soon carrying whole pages of prosecutions for blackout offences.

The authorities could be equally zealous in their enforcement of the regulations. In one case, a policeman, unable to gain access to a property to turn the offending lights off, called in a police marksman to shoot them out through a grille. The offending property-owner later had insult added to injury with a £2 fine. There were also unexpected side effects of the blackout. For one thing, there was nowhere to sit down. Local authorities, fearful that pedestrians would trip over wayside seats in the darkness and sue the council, started uprooting them, leading to protests from elderly residents. Ingenious plans, such as reinstalling them in the private gardens of public-spirited citizens, were floated.

Drowning or tripping over seats were not the only dangers facing the habitués of the blackout. A Dover man was fined 5s for what was intriguingly but imprecisely described in court as 'committing a nuisance' in Market Lane. Police told the court that they had had 'considerable difficulty with such offences' since the blackout had been introduced.

But not everyone was passionate about the blackout:

> *A good deal of indignation was expressed to the* Observer *over the extinguishing of the Front Line illuminations and those at Alexandra Park, as well as the general reduction of lighting in the streets. Correspondents declared that this was creating an unnecessary atmosphere of war panic, particularly in the minds of elderly people, and this was doing as much to harm the holiday season by scaring people as the crisis itself. They argue that the lights could surely be switched off in an instant if the need arises, and it was reprehensible to aggravate an already grave situation by carrying precautions to such an apparently absurd length.* Hastings and St Leonards Observer, 2 September 1939

The Council shrugged their corporate shoulders and said they were just following Home Office instructions. However, the most spectacular breach of the blackout was later to occur in Hastings in July 1940, courtesy of the local police force. They had confiscated a large quantity of fireworks from local retailers under the Defence of the Realm Regulations and had scheduled them for destruction. In the early hours of one July morning, the local residents all leapt from their beds, thinking a major air raid was in progress. The fireworks, which were being stored in the yard of the police station, had somehow caught fire and the town was treated to the largest and least premeditated firework display of the war.

People got used to seeing military vehicles in the streets around them. These tanks are carrying out an exercise at Goudhurst.

The coastal towns very soon became areas under military occupation. As early as May 1938, the Medway towns had witnessed a major Civil Defence exercise, with planes from RAF Manston simulating bombing raids. There were also major pre-war army exercises:

> [The] *heaviest troop movements since the war* [i.e., that of 1914-18] *were witnessed in Maidstone and the Medway towns on Saturday. During the night and almost continuously on Friday morning, lorries of steel-helmeted soldiers, machine gun carriers, light lorries with Bren and anti-tank guns mounted on them, were passing through the town. At times there was as many as twenty army vehicles in High Street, giving the town a very military aspect.*
>
> *The troops aroused a great deal of interest and many took snaps of them as they passed. The soldiers waved to girls in shops and offices.* Kent Messenger, 26 August 1939

Among the first to be called up were the women volunteers of the ATS (Auxiliary Territorial Service), who were told to report to Maidstone Depot. The local press was typically (for the day) condescending about the ladies' contribution to the war effort:

'We keep saluting the wrong people and making other awful mistakes but we have not been court-martialled yet' said Volunteer Whiffen. 'They are a jolly fine crowd of soldiers and are ready to forgive us for whatever we do.' Kent Messenger, 2 September 1939

The biggest danger to their physical wellbeing was apparently the risk of them spraining their delicate little wrists lifting the pint mugs from which the soldiers drank their tea. As for moral dangers:

Language is causing the regular soldiers a certain amount of trouble. By the exercise of almost superhuman control... the officers and NCOs do their best to spare the ATS volunteers' blushes. Kent Messenger, 2 September 1939

Any large unoccupied houses were liable to be requisitioned and filled with soldiers. Armed guards waited at arrival points like railway and bus stations to check the papers of new arrivals. Soldiers with fixed bayonets patrolled the streets and the military were not even allowed any respite in their leisure time:

Soldiers were ordered to carry their tin hats, rifles and gas masks wherever they went; this caused some problems when they attempted to squeeze along between the rows of seats in the local cinemas. Often the 'Alert' slide would suddenly flash up on the screen and then we would have to leave in a hurry. Roy Humphreys. *Hellfire Corner: Reminiscences of Wartime in South East England*, Sutton, 1994, p. 6

But there were fears that some of the military personnel could end up in less desirable places. Young servicemen were 'often lured to places where they had more drink than was good for them.' To counter this, the Salvation Army opened a rest and recreation centre for members of the forces in Snargate Street, Dover, within weeks of the start of the war. The Army 'was not out to ram religion down the service man's throat, but to supply their temporal needs and create that atmosphere which was helpful to them.' They provided reading, writing and recreation rooms and a cafeteria. In their view 'places like the Institute were very badly needed in Dover, especially in the vicinity of the docks.'

The Royal Hippodrome in Dover was probably one of the places the Salvation Army were warning about. But their temptations did not stop at the demon drink. As the war got under way, they advertised a stream of titillating entertainments that many a soldier's mother would not have wanted their boy exposed to:

The most talked-of girl in England! Drina, the modern Venus from the Folies Bergere, Paris. Drina glories the female form, unadorned. Advertisement in the *Dover Express and East Kent News*, 13 October 1939

One of the inseparable companions of warfare, rumour, was quick to rear its head. Very early on in the hostilities, the Admiralty found it necessary to quash stories that were circulating in the area:

There is no foundation whatsoever for the many rumours which have been in circulation during the last few days respecting the loss of various capital ships, in particular His Majesty's Ships Hood, Renown and Repulse. These stories are lying and baseless rumours, designed to alarm and depress the public, and those who spread them are doing a gross disservice to their country. Dover Express and East Kent News, 22 September 1939

The Ministry of Information also found it necessary within weeks of the outbreak of war to set up Voluntary Local Information Committees, to counteract the proliferation of rumours. But they were fighting a losing battle. Nothing seemed too improbable to feed the rumour mill. When Maidstone's water supply suffered temporary discoloration as a result of engineering works, word spread that Hitler had poisoned the supply. Those who hoped that rumour would be countered by

The war-weary of Dover could seek diversion in an 'Artistic Nude Presentation – The Bridal Morn',

the authorities providing full information were in for a disappointment. The editor of the *Dover Express* declared baldly at the outset of hostilities that Dover was prepared for war, and went on:

> *Those who expect to find any records of details of preparations at Dover in the press will be disappointed. No Defence of the Realm Regulations will be necessary to prevent the publication of information that will be of use to any enemy.* Dover Express and East Kent News, 15 September 1939

It became one of that particular newspaper's themes to rail against what they saw as information of use to an enemy that was being supplied by the national newspapers and, in particular, the BBC, to the enemy. To some extent, their complaints were understandable. Press reports that most of the shells from the German long-distance artillery aimed at Dover were falling short might well have helped the Germans to find their range (though the same information might have been obtained through a telescope). But their objections to reports that delivery of Home Guard tin helmets was being delayed were perhaps a little over-sensitive, as was the editorial view that 'the BBC should be abolished except for the dissemination of British military band music.'

This was a snapshot of life in some of the communities of Kent and Sussex at the outbreak of war. A more systematic picture of public attitudes is provided by the Gallup polls conducted in the early stages of the war. Those in September 1939 showed a small majority of the national population (54 per cent) believing that the war would be over in less than three months. Eighty-nine per cent believed that we should continue to prosecute the war until Hitler was ousted and 84 per cent believed we would be victorious. But right up to December 1939, the Government in general (61 per cent) and Chamberlain personally (64 per cent) had the support of a majority of the public for the half-hearted way they were conducting the war. In a straight fight for public support between Chamberlain and Churchill, Chamberlain would have been the clear winner (52 to 30, the polls predicted).

But for several months the British people would see little of what the war really meant. The 'Phoney War' was the story of a thousand small irritations and few real dramas. Nor was the preparedness of our armed forces tested in any way. Had they been able to see the truth about the state of their armed forces, how afraid would the people of Kent and Sussex have been?

Chapter Two

Ready or not, here we come

In September 1939 the British Army was totally unfit to fight a first-class war on the continent of Europe... In the years preceding the outbreak of war no large-scale exercises with troops had been held in England for some time. Indeed, the Regular Army was unfit to take part in a realistic exercise... It must be said to our shame that we sent our army into that most modern war with weapons and equipment that were quite inadequate, and we had only ourselves to blame for the disasters which early overtook us in the field when fighting began in 1940. Field Marshal Bernard Montgomery, Memoirs, Collins, 1958, pp. 49-50

An expensive motor car, beautifully polished, complete in every detail, except that there is no petrol in the tank. A J P Taylor on British war preparations in 1939, quoted in Nicholas Bethell, *The War Hitler Won*, Allen Lane, 1972, p. 85

Before the war

Britain after 1918 was a nation haunted by the horrors of war. In the years up to 1939, successive British governments recoiled at the prospect of further armed conflict in Europe. Home Secretary Samuel Hoare summed up the feelings of many when he told the Cabinet:

I view the prospect of the despatch of a field force to France with the greatest misgivings. We should need, at any rate in the initial stages, all our available troops to assist in the defence of this country. 11 April 1938: Richard Lamb. *The Drift to War 1922-39*, W H Allen, 1989, p. 291

For much of the period, the Treasury insisted that the services plan on the assumption that there would be no war within ten years. During the 1930s successive War Ministers tried to get the Government to invest in modernising the army, but they faced implacable opposition, not least from Neville Chamberlain, first as Chancellor of the Exchequer and then as Prime Minister:

The political temper of people in this country [is] *strongly opposed to continental adventures and suspicious of any preparations made in peace time with a view to large-scale military operations on the continent... Our aim should be to deter war and that might be better done by increasing the air force.* Cabinet papers 53/29 and 23/86: Chamberlain, quoted in Lamb

The Royal Air Force in 1938 was far from ready to take on the Luftwaffe. Of the twenty-nine squadrons considered to be ready for mobilisation, only five were equipped with modern aircraft. Five of the squadrons were equipped with Gladiators, a biplane fighter that only came into service in 1937, but which was already hopelessly out-paced and out-gunned by the opposition. Even at the time

Chaotic scenes, as members of the British Expeditionary Force set out for France in early May 1940. Many – the lucky ones – would soon be back.

of its introduction, this fighter was slower than the Germans' Ju88 bomber. Other squadrons were even worse-equipped. This did not stop Chamberlain describing the strike capability of the Royal Air Force in glowing terms:

> *This enormous power, this almost terrifying power which Britain is building up has a sobering effect, a steadying effect on the opinion of the world.* 7 March 1938: Lamb, p. 293

Nor was the aircraft industry geared up for the kind of rapid growth the Government belatedly proposed for the air force. In 1938, at a time when the amount of labour required to build an aircraft was about ten times that needed for the planes of 1914-18, it employed just over a quarter of the numbers it had at the peak of the First World War. Fortunately, a marked upswing in production began from the latter part of 1938.

In the view of the army, the expansion of the air force was paid for at their expense. The most obvious manifestation of this was a Cabinet Memorandum of 16 February 1938, proposing a new role for the army that focussed primarily upon anti-aircraft defence, with two Territorial divisions being wholly given over to those duties. The army was disgusted: 'The White Paper is truly the most appalling reading,' General (later Sir) Edmund Ironside (the future Commander in Chief of the Home Forces) wrote in his diary. Even after Munich, when Chamberlain told the Commons of the urgent need to re-arm Britain, there was no significant extra money for the army. Right up until February 1939, Britain insisted that its contribution to any continental Expeditionary Force would be limited to two divisions. This, and the outrage it caused in France, was not lost upon Hitler.

Even when the occupation of Czechoslovakia forced the Government into serious re-armament, they made the wrong choices. Chamberlain's fear of conscription led to him double the size of the Territorial Army, at a cost of £88 millions, but this had the effect of diverting arms and equipment away from the front-line troops, and diluted the ratio of armour to infantry.

The navy still had a large numerical supremacy over the Germans, but it too had been badly neglected between the wars. When Churchill returned as First Sea Lord of the Admiralty in 1939, most of the ships under his command had been laid down during his previous tenure of that post, in 1911-15.

The British Expeditionary Force
But once war was declared, the British Expeditionary Force set off cheerfully for France. By March 1940 almost a quarter of a million men had crossed the Channel. There were ten divisions, the flower of the British Army, but also some who were

If you wanted to be a soldier with a weapon in 1940, all you had to do was to find an armed member of the enemy and take his. Here, troops are shown how.

a considerable way short of blossoming. Over half of the force consisted of non-combat troops, designed to pave the way for the fighting reinforcements that were to follow them. The entire force had less than fifty heavy tanks for infantry support, just about a hundred medium tanks for deep penetration and several hundred light tanks, which were only suitable for reconnaissance and helpless when confronted by German armour.

Many of the divisions were under-trained and under-equipped. In one account of those days, a member of 68 Field Regiment, Royal Artillery, recalls the motley assortment of furniture vans, coal wagons and other vehicles requisitioned to tow their antique wooden-wheeled field guns, dating from the First World War. The then twenty-year-old Thomas Jones had been called up from the Territorials and, a fortnight before beginning the retreat to Dunkirk, had been working at home on the farm. Another soldier's recollection of his unit, one of the last to join the BEF, further illustrates the problem:

*It was with this travesty of an armoured division – a formation with less than half its proper armoured strength, without any field guns or a proper complement of anti-tank and anti-aircraft guns, without infantry, without air support, without the bulk of its ancillary services, and with part of its headquarters in a three-ply wooden 'armoured' command vehicle – that I was ordered to force a crossing over a defended, unfordable river, and afterwards to advance some sixty miles, through four **real** armoured divisions, to the help of the British Expeditionary Force.* Joan Bright. *The 9th Queen's Royal Lancers, 1936-1945*, Aldershot, 1951

Equipment shortages were not helped by an active black market operated by members of the force themselves. Hayward records that this grew to be such a problem that the War Office had to despatch 500 staff with police experience to France to deal with it. In addition to shortages of equipment and training, the British were woefully deficient in tactical terms. Between the wars, British military strategists like Lieutenant Colonel John Fuller and Captain Basil Liddell Hart had set out most of the principles of blitzkrieg, the tank-based war of rapid movement that the Germans were about to unleash on Europe, but they were prophets without honour in their own country. Their books found many more readers in Germany, not least the great tank commander Heinz Guderian, when still just a captain in the German army. Instead of learning the lessons of the Polish campaign, the British Expeditionary Force spent much of their first winter in France trying to replicate the static defences of the Maginot Line along their section of the front and exercising in the semi-ruined trenches of the First World War – preparing for the last war, rather than the one that was about to come:

We dug a lot, latrines and gun pits, in that order, and we did have one movement exercise on the insistence of the second-in-command who was a First World War veteran. This was pretty disastrous: it was at night and many got lost. It did not augur well... Lance Bombardier Peter Lambert of the BEF, quoted in R A C Parker. *The Second World War*, Oxford UP, 1989, p. 10

The French had the largest army in the world, and were able to put 102 divisions into the field. In these circumstances, it was small wonder that the BEF was placed under the overall command of the French. This was to prove disastrous for the British, who were dogged throughout the campaign by a lack of co-ordination and co-operation between the armies, and by the staggering incompetence of the French High Command under General Gamelin. They issued the BEF with incomprehensible, often conflicting and sometimes downright suicidal orders that flew in the face of the reality on the ground:

> *The ineptitude of the French Higher Command was so great that it seemed that it could only be explained by treachery. The Russians would have shot most of the generals in similar circumstances.* Philip Warner. *The Battle of France 1940,* Cassell, 1990, p. 67

The Germans' rapid destruction of the Polish armed forces in the first days of war gave an ominous warning both of their power and of the changing nature of warfare. The British strategy, which laid greater emphasis on naval power and the more static lines of land defence, no longer held good in the days of the tank, the submarine and the aeroplane. But it was early naval reverses, like the successful German attacks on Scapa Flow and the Firth of Forth, that gave Britain the first uncomfortable message that they were less secure in their island fortress than they had previously thought.

The final result – that Poland was overrun within a month – does not tell the full story. The campaign revealed significant cracks in the German war machine, as

The 25-pounder field gun, one of the many items in short supply to the British Expeditionary Force.

well as its strengths. Their panzers out-distanced both their infantry and their supply lines, and they left themselves stranded and vulnerable to attack even from the Poles' enfeebled bomber forces. It also highlighted the limitations of the tank in urban street-fighting. In one three-hour engagement, Polish defenders destroyed no less than fifty-seven German tanks, using anti-tank guns and Molotov cocktails. Meanwhile in the west, the Allies boasted (in *The Times* of 3 October) that they had occupied some 100,000 acres of German territory. To bring this down to reality, it represents about 156 square miles (or 484 million square yards, if that sounds bigger). Some much more substantial territorial gains were about to be made in that theatre of war, not all of them necessarily to the advantage of the Allies.

When the onslaught in the west finally came, on 10 May 1940, Gamelin, rather than allow the BEF to benefit from the positions they had spent the winter busily fortifying, ordered them forward, deep into Belgium. The British expected to find an equally strong defensive line prepared, but found to their horror that the line along the River Dyle was almost totally undefended. Their rapid advance was followed by an equally rapid retreat back to their prepared lines. These turned out to delay, rather than repulse, the Germans. As for the 'impregnable' defences of their allies, the Germans landed a dozen or so gliders on the roof of the fortress of Eben Emael in Belgium, and captured it within hours at a cost of twenty-one casualties. The Maginot Line they simply went around, through the Ardennes (again, a tactic anticipated by Basil Liddell Hart).

The Dunkirk evacuation was originally conceived as a means of removing all the non-essential, non-combat troops – all the 'useless mouths' – from the battlefield; to leave all the rations and other supplies to the fighting men. It went on for several days in that form, before turning into the full-scale evacuation that it became. Even so, many of these non-combat troops found themselves thrust into combat situations, and some acquitted themselves very well – a crucial bridge was held by a force comprised entirely of padres (who no doubt looked beyond the air force in seeking support from above) and a mobile bath unit, which found itself even more exposed than its customers.

Then came one of the most mysterious decisions of the war – Hitler's order to the panzers to halt, just as they were tightening the noose around Dunkirk, and to leave the final destruction of the BEF to the Luftwaffe. Several theories have been advanced for this, though none has been conclusively proven:

- that the panzers were long overdue for service (which was true) and could have faltered, due to mechanical failure;
- related to this, that Hitler wanted to save the panzers for his main objective, the defeat of France;
- that the terrain around Dunkirk (part-flooded and crossed with waterways) did not lend itself to tank operation;
- that the panzers' over-extended flanks were exposed to a possible French counter-attack (possible, but it was never going to happen – even the Germans overestimated the competence of the French generals);
- that Hitler wanted Britain to have an opportunity to make an honourable peace;

- that Hitler believed Goering's boasts, that his Luftwaffe was the best way to destroy the remainder of the BEF;
- that Hitler did not want the German army to take all the credit for destroying the British Army, and preferred to see the glory go to the more ideologically reliable Goering.

Dunkirk – as seen from England

This was not an army in defeat. This was an army that expressed itself in these terms. 'We haven't started yet. Give us a bit of sleep and a brush up and let's get back. We'll get the Huns next time. Kent and Sussex Courier, 7 June 1940

I would like to make it quite clear here that the whole time I was in France, I never knew where I was, where I was going or what I was doing – hardly anybody did, and the top brass wanted it that way. Corporal Jim Peall of the British Expeditionary Force, quoted in David J Knowles. *With Resolve, with Valour,* Knowles, 2002, p. 27

The south coast began to see refugees well before the evacuation of Dunkirk began. A Belgian steam tug, crowded with Belgian and French refugees, was towed in to dock at Hastings in May 1940. A band played 'Tipperary' as they came ashore and the assembled crowd cheered heartily, but the refugees were in no fit state for a big welcome:

Among them were elderly men, women, young girls and little children, all sea-soaked and looking wan and haggard from fatigue, exposure and hunger. Many

Members of the British Expeditionary Force arrive back from Dunkirk in little ships. In fact, most travelled back with the Royal Navy.

Headcorn station, where many of the packed trainloads of Dunkirk evacuees were fed and watered.

> *were from Liege and Brussels and were still carrying bundles of personal belongings they had snatched from their homes ten days before. Nearly all of them had tales to tell of pitiless machine-gunning by enemy aircraft of trains and cars carrying refugees to safety. Hastings and St Leonards Observer, 25 May 1940*

Among them were two who were carrying more than personal valuables. The Finance Director and Chief Engineer of the Belgian Railway had two suitcases filled with 13 million Belgian francs, the entire reserves of their national railway.

They said it was to ensure that the railway employees could have a pay-day, 'as soon as arrangements could be made'. Pay-day may have been some time off.

From late May, the sounds of the battle in France could be heard from Kent, but people at home did not realise how badly things were going for the Expeditionary Force. A military expert, invited to address the meeting of the Hastings branch of the Primrose League in late May 1940 gave the following confident prediction:

Soon we shall find it is not a case of the Germans being halted, but they will be falling back... They have had tremendous losses, while we not only have our main forces still intact, but we have the men of the whole of the British Empire pouring in to help us. Hastings and St Leonards Observer, 25 May 1940

Even as he spoke, the men of the British Expeditionary Force were crowding onto the beaches and harbour at Dunkirk, with only a miracle standing between them and capture or death. But their would-be rescuers were assembling across the water, and other preparations for their return were being made. The secrecy surrounding the evacuation did not help the emergency services to prepare. All they were told was that something had gone wrong over the other side. It was not clear from this whether they were preparing for an evacuation or an invasion. Eastbourne Pier had the explosives that were strapped to it hurriedly disconnected when it became clear that the next people to use the pier were likely to be the British Expeditionary Force, rather than the Germans.

A local reporter described the scene at an unnamed departure port (probably Dover) as the rescue got under way:

The port of departure had the appearance of a regatta day, both ashore and afloat, with a grim reminder every now and again that something more serious was afoot. Fishing boats from every port on the south and east coasts crowded the harbour. The fleet of lifeboats added a gay touch of colour. There were pleasure boats, paddle steamers, 'sixpenny sick' craft from Southend, complete with drinking bars, Thames barges under sail and tow [and] yachts... Ashore the crew swarmed about the naval headquarters, discussing the job ahead, the weather, the tides and their chances. Old shipmates from distant ports met with a handshake. It all seemed much more like a regatta than a war... until one saw the destroyers that came limping or hurrying into harbour, their decks a solid mass of waving khaki. Wounded men and wounded ships sharply cancelled the regatta atmosphere.

The men in khaki – French, Belgian and British – tramped wearily along the jetties where they were landed, almost – but not quite – too exhausted to smile. The heroic deeds performed by the navy could be read by those who knew how to interpret the signs of the port. Officers, wearing soaked uniforms, hollow-eyed from lack of sleep. Bluejackets tumbling cheerfully into small, unfamiliar, commandeered craft to set out on the 45 mile crossing to the opposite coast. Destroyers, funnels, bridges and boats riddled with bullet holes, listing dangerously through flooded compartments, running to and fro five or six times a day, and perhaps more, just as though they were on a ferry service. Hastings and St Leonards Observer, 8 June 1940

The evacuees arrived on stretchers; they arrived covered in oil; they arrived dressed in rags or naked, wrapped in blankets. Even in these circumstances, the incoming soldiers all had to be identified and checked by immigration. Those who had returned with nothing were in some difficulty in proving their identity, and some suspicious cases were arrested.

According to some Dunkirk evacuees, the most striking sight on disembarkation from their journey from hell was seeing the civilian population queuing for the cinema, walking about with tennis or golf equipment, and generally behaving as if there were no war within a million miles of them. The same nonchalance was reflected in the local newspapers. In the midst of the drama of the retreat to Dunkirk, some correspondents were much more concerned about the amenities of their seafront. One wrote to complain about Hastings Parade being 'disfigured' by the 'sad and ageing women' carrying 'stop the war' placards. Another was concerned about eyesores of a rather more earthy kind:

Dear Sir,

On Thursday 16 May, at midday, a young woman with the least possible covering was sprawling on a seat and on a young man in Warrior Square Gardens. A disgusting sight, as she had massive limbs.

Sunbathing should only be allowed on the beach, and young women with the shortest of shorts and only a handkerchief in front should not be allowed on the promenade, or streets, or in public gardens.

These immodest persons are a danger and should be suppressed. Letter to the Hastings and St Leonards Observer, 25 May 1940

But others were only too keenly aware of events across the Channel. In the newspapers over the following weeks, readers relived the harrowing tales of those who had escaped and the desperate hopes of the families whose loved ones were still missing:

His wife has not given up hope of the possibility that he is safe, and will not believe him dead until after the war. She is almost certain of his return. The family base their hope of Harry's safety on the fact that nearly every member of his battalion has been reported missing.

Teams of volunteers worked around the clock, preparing food for the forces returning from Dunkirk. Some were allegedly put off sandwiches for life by the experience.

The Southern Railway played a heroic, if not widely celebrated, role in the evacuation. First, they were at the time also a substantial shipping operator, and sent forty-two ships (cross-Channel and Isle of Wight ferries and general cargo vessels) to Dunkirk. Twelve of them were lost.

But more miraculous than heroic was the operation the Southern Railway and the other public transport services staged to move the evacuated forces from the British coast to their eventual destinations. They only received details of Operation *Dynamo* (the evacuation plan) at 5.00 pm on the evening of Sunday, 26 May; the operation started the following dawn. There was no indication of how many troops would need transporting (early estimates suggested about a tenth of the 338,000 final number) or of which ports they would be landing in, so no serious advance planning was possible even in those few hours.

In the end, seven main ports were used, from Margate to Southampton. All the nation's railway companies had to be mobilised to provide the locomotives and carriages required – about 2,000 items of rolling stock – all of which had to be directed on an *ad hoc* basis (by telephone) to different ports as new arrivals were spotted. If the point of arrival was complicated, their destinations were complex in the extreme, with troops being sent all over the country. Many of the French evacuees, for example, had to be returned to France via Plymouth.

Most of the men had not eaten or slept for days, and feeding centres had to be speedily improvised at key railway stations – Headcorn, Faversham and Paddock Wood. At Headcorn, forty soldiers and between forty and fifty local women, working up to twelve-hour shifts, served food to up to eight hundred exhausted men on a train in as little as eight minutes. They drank their tea out of tin cans and threw them out of the window for re-use as the train pulled out. Food was prepared in biblical quantities – 50,000lb of bread a day was baked on site and another 50,000lb brought in; 5,000 eggs were prepared at a sitting; meat was cooked over huge trench fires on improvised spits, and a million sardines were consumed. At the same time, postcards were handed out, for the men to write and give to people waiting at the next station, informing their families that they were safe. Clothes were found for those in most desperate need; some civilian passengers gave them items from their own luggage. The Dreamland amusement arcade in Margate became a clothing store, serving several thousand men a day as Kent and Sussex were scoured for spare clothing. All this as crowds of anxious relatives thronged the platform and trackside, seeking news, or better, sight, of their sons or husbands.

But, for all the patriotism and the propaganda, nothing could disguise the fact that this was a major defeat. Molly Panter-Downes, reporting in *The New Yorker* magazine on a June 1940 Gallup poll, saying only 3 per cent of the British public believed they might lose the war, observed that 'it would be difficult for an impartial observer to decide today whether the British are the bravest or merely the most stupid people in the world... Perhaps it's a lack of imagination.'

Britain was militarily naked and near-bankrupt. According to Barnett, some estimates showed that Britain's financial reserves – and with them, her capacity to wage war – would be exhausted before the end of 1940. Nor was even the best-informed of Britons able to predict with any confidence what the Germans' next move would be:

Twice in two months we had been taken completely by surprise. The overrunning of Norway and the breakthrough at Sedan, with all that followed from these, proved the deadly power of the German initiative. What else had they got ready – prepared and organised to the last inch? Would they suddenly pounce out of the blue with new weapons, perfect planning and overwhelming force upon our almost totally unequipped and disarmed Island at any one of a dozen or a score of possible landing places?... He would have been a very foolish man who allowed his reasoning, however clean-cut and seemingly sure, to blot out any possibility against which provision could be made. Winston S Churchill. *The Second World War, Vol. II – Their Finest Hour,* Guild, 1949, p. 143

But as one army was returning home in disarray, another was being created with quite breathtaking speed.

Chapter Three

Stay put – and take one with you

Just let them come! The Germans are dropping troops by parachute. It is possible that they will attempt to do this here as well! I speak for thousands, if not millions, of former soldiers who all know how to shoot. We are too old for active service, but we can handle a gun! Just let them come!' Letter to the editor of the *News of the World*, featured on its front page, 12 May 1940

If the night is a little misty, the first big battle on English soil will probably be fought out between the British Army and the LDV. Unnamed British Army officer, 6 July 1940

Stay put...

The civilian population of the coastal areas presented a potentially severe problem for those defending the coast. In continental Europe, the chaotic floods of refugees clogging up the roads had played havoc with Allied attempts to conduct a defensive war. By the middle of July, about two-fifths of the coastal population of Kent, some 80,000 people, had been evacuated inland (or had evacuated themselves), and similar large-scale movements of population took place along the East Anglian coast and other threatened areas.

The rest were told to stay put if invasion came, until such time as an official evacuation, under Government control, was ordered. In two memoranda on 4 and 5 July, Churchill told his Chief of Staff, General Ismay, to take steps to avoid the chaos seen on the continent, in the event of the Germans landing:

What is being done to encourage and assist the people living in threatened seaports to make suitable shelters for themselves in which they could remain during an invasion? Active measures must be taken forthwith. Officers or representatives of the local authority should go round explaining to families that if they decide not to leave in accordance with our general advice, they should remain in the cellars, and arrangements should be made to prop up the building overhead. They should be assisted in this both with advice and materials. Their gas masks should be inspected. All this must be put actively in operation from today. This process will stimulate voluntary evacuation, and at the same time make reasonable provision for those who remain.

Clear instruction should now be issued about the people living in the threatened coastal zones: (1) They should be encouraged as much as possible to depart voluntarily, both by the pressure of a potential compulsory order hanging over them, and also by local (not national) propaganda through their Regional Commissioners or local bodies. Those who wish to stay, or can find nowhere to go on their own, should be told that if invasion impact occurs in their town or village on the coast they will not be able to leave till the battle is over. They should therefore be encouraged and helped to put their cellars in order so that they have fairly safe places to go to. They should be supplied with whatever form of Anderson shelter is now available... Only those who are trustworthy should be allowed to stay. All doubtful elements should be removed.

Pray have precise proposals formulated upon these lines for my approval.

Churchill, pp. 235-6

Wide-ranging measures were also put in place to deny the invaders essential supplies. Many petrol pumps were removed in coastal areas, and plans were made to ensure that the rest were destroyed, or would have the storage tanks filled with water, to render them unusable in an emergency. Leaflets were sent out to all households, telling them to deny access to food and other essentials to the invaders. Cars and other forms of transport were to be immobilised.

The Germans also recognised the importance of the chaos a retreating civilian population could cause for the defending forces. Their propaganda radio stations deliberately broadcast misleading instructions, designed to maximise confusion in the event of an invasion. They told the British population to ignore their Government's cynical instruction to 'stay put' when invasion came. Instead, they were told to head for the hills (specifically, those far-removed hills of North Wales and north-west Scotland, in order to maximise confusion). They also warned of a range of terror weapons, which were variously:

- *true* (the 'flying torpedoes' they forecast in August 1940 materialised as the V1s four years later);
- *speculative* (their high-speed landing craft with aeroplane engines were tried but could not be made to work) and;
- *pure nonsense* (fog pills).

They sought to spread alarm as widely as possible among the population, at various times forecasting invasion in as many as twenty different locations. They gave misinformation as to when the tides and moon were favourable for landings, and identified other events (such as the shelling of Dover and the bombing of the railway line from London to Ramsgate/Folkestone) as presaging landings in those areas. At one point, after shelling, they declared Dover to be 'already practically German territory'.

They also capitalised on the hysteria over the fifth column. False messages, in an easily broken code, were broadcast to non-existent agents in Britain and, on the night of 13/14 August, several groups of parachutes and other equipment were dropped in various parts of Britain, in an effort to add to the view that the country was being overrun by fifth columnists. This was given considerable coverage by German-run New British Broadcasting Station, in the hope that it would be impossible for the British to prove that nobody had actually landed. Unfortunately for the Germans, some of the equipment fell among standing corn, and the absence of tracks leading from the 'abandoned' parachutes exposed the lie.

For a time, some of the German broadcasts attracted huge listening figures (helped not a little by the feeble nature of the BBC's output during the early stages of the war, and by the national press publishing the times and frequencies of the German broadcasts). A Ministry of Information survey in January 1940 estimated that 26 per cent of the British public had listened to Lord Haw-Haw in the previous twenty-four hours. The authorities were worried, and the BBC even entered into a ratings war, moving their most popular programmes around to try and reduce the numbers listening to propaganda.

The Home Guard – the Last Desperate Venture

The battered survivors of the British Expeditionary Force were licking their wounds, at home on seven days' leave, or in hospital. Their tanks, guns and other equipment littered the roads and beaches of northern France. Now, old men, youths, people in reserved occupations – anyone, in the words of the recruitment material 'capable of free movement' – were being called upon to volunteer for a new military force. Their official name at the outset was the LDV, the Local Defence Volunteers, but their nickname – the 'Last Desperate Venture' – spoke volumes about Britain's state of preparedness to resist the so-far invincible Nazi war machine. They were formed, following a broadcast by the Secretary of State for War, Anthony Eden, on 14 May 1940, inviting people to volunteer at their local police stations (the police had not been properly forewarned about this, and certainly were not prepared for the scale of the response they would receive. They rapidly rejected any suggestion that they should play any part in organising this new service, beyond collecting the names).

An armoured personnel carrier rattles its way up Cranbrook High Street.

The Weapons of the Home Guard

A Home Guard weapon was one that was dangerous to the enemy, and, to a greater degree, to the operator.
Lieutenant Colonel J Lee, Commander of a Home Guard Battalion

The Government was swamped by applications to join the Home Guard and, by the end of September 1940, only just over half of them were armed (740,000 out of 1,682,000 recruits were still without weapons). What was needed were weapons that were cheap and easy to manufacture in large numbers. British (and a little foreign) ingenuity soon came to the rescue, with varying results:

Weapons of the Home Guard 1: Death by throwing – the No. 76 Self-Igniting Phosphorous (SIP) Grenade

Better known to you and I as the Molotov cocktail, this was the first time such a weapon had been put in even semi-official military hands. It comprised a half-pint glass bottle, filled with phosphorus, benzine and latex, which caught fire when the glass was broken. The latex was to make the grenade's contents stick to the target when it burst. Therein lay the first problem; the glass often did not break when thrown. It needed to be dropped from a height of at least eight feet onto concrete. Having broken, its poisonous fumes could choke the thrower, if the wind were in the wrong direction. However, as with many of these weapons, a good deal of propaganda was put about concerning their war-winning qualities. 'Six of these breaking on a tank one after the other should cause sufficient heat and smoke to bring the crew out,' claimed the instructions of the day. Over six million had been distributed to the Home Guard by August 1941. There were two kinds; the red-capped version was designed to be thrown, whereas the green ones could be fired from the Northover Projector.

The idea was far from being the brainchild of Anthony Eden. Even before the outbreak of war, there were efforts being made to get older ex-military men back into uniform:

Recruits wanted for the National Defence Companies: Ex-servicemen between the ages of 45 and 55 are urgently needed for the National Defence Companies, and they are wanted now. The duties are to act as guards at the various vulnerable points in the county, such as railway bridges, important traffic centres and many other points which, if attacked by an enemy agent would endanger the efficient action of the armies in the field. Just as the army must have its Supply Corps to feed it and supply the munitions and other equipment, so that protection must be provided for the stores and communications at home, since the damage to any of these would at once be felt in the holding up of transport or the shortage of necessary supplies in the field. Advertisement in Hastings and St Leonards Observer, 2 September 1939

Even though they were being asked to perform many of the same duties subsequently given to the Home Guard, these were full-time posts with regular army rates of pay and allowances.

Churchill had been lobbying Hore-Belisha (the War Minister) since October 1939 to set up a 'Home Guard' (he had proposed that name from the outset), and a completely independent 'League of Frontiersmen' had been established in Essex at about the same time. Press baron Lord Kemsley was using his newspapers to call for something similar and was even offering to fund it himself. His views were being supported in both Houses of Parliament. In deepest Herefordshire, Lady Helena Gleichen took direct action: she organised her staff and tenants into an irregular force to defend the ancestral home at Much Marcle and wrote to her local branch of the army, demanding rifles, ammunition and 'a couple of machine guns, if you have any'. Territorial Associations, struggling to find a role, also lobbied for local volunteer forces.

The regular army was horrified at the prospect of these bands of unlicensed Davy Crocketts roaming the countryside. General Ironside warned that:

> *armed civilians acting independently might well upset the plans of a military commander by their unexpected and unorganised activities. He added that action was needed before civilian residents on the east coast took the law into their own hands and formed their own private defence bands.* General Staff Officer to C-in-C Home Forces, quoted in S P Mackenzie, *The Home Guard*, Oxford UP, 1995, p. 29.

The establishment of the Home Guard can therefore be seen as less a reasoned policy decision and more an attempt to impose order on the threat of chaos.

In Kent, an estimated 10,000 men enrolled within the twenty-four hours following Eden's speech. Within days, Brighton had over 1,500 and Worthing over 1,000 LDV volunteers enrolled; Eastbourne had over 900, Shoreham and Southwick about 300 (not all of them under sixty-five), and Tunbridge Wells and Horsham around 500 each, including some Boer War veterans. Haywards Heath had recruited 300, Burgess Hill 150 and Hurstpierpoint 120. In total, Sussex had almost 9,000 'parashooters', as the local paper had decided to christen them, within days. Some were quite open about breaching the age limit – the entire sixth form of The King's School in Canterbury registered en masse and smaller boys attempted to pass themselves off as seventeen. At the other end of the scale, many recruits had been refused military service during the First World War on account of being over-age even then. Former Regimental Sergeant Major Hugh Pakenham presented himself at Brighton police station and demanded an enrolment form, despite admitting to being seventy-five years old: 'But I'm sound in wind and limb, and why shouldn't I join?' he demanded. They gave him a form. Another ex-army recruit arrived at Bromley bedecked in his campaign medals. Asked his age, he replied 'Sixty-three'. The questioner pointed out that that would have made him about ten years old when he won his medal for the Chitral campaign (1892-1902).

By the end of the month, around 300,000 people nationwide had signed up and by August it had passed a million, far surpassing Eden's expectations when he

---

Weapons of the Home Guard 2: Gelignite in a Tin
The No. 73 Grenade was popularly known as the Woolworth, or Thermos, Bomb, it comprised 'just a lump of gelignite in a biscuit tin'. It was heavy, and hard to throw far enough to avoid putting the thrower in danger. But the explosion it made was nothing, if not spectacular.

Weapons of the Home Guard 3: Sticky Socks

The No. 74 Grenade, or Sticky Bomb, had previously been developed for, and rejected by, the army as an anti-tank weapon. Another glass container, this time filled with nitro-glycerine, was covered with a sock and coated with an adhesive. It was prone to leaking and breaking, and would not stick to anything wet or muddy (which included most tanks). It would, however, stick firmly to anyone throwing it, if it brushed their clothes, and with fatal results. The army assessors concluded that 'the whole article is most objectionable', but Churchill ordered the manufacture of a million, for distribution to the Home Guard.

made the speech. Initially there were only weapons for a fraction of them, no uniforms and no organisational structure. The police ran out of enrolment forms and, once completed, these had to be given to 'a properly appointed commander' – the only problem being that there were no such commanders appointed and no mechanism for appointing them. The Lords Lieutenant of the counties were brought in to resolve this impasse, and they worked with the senior military commanders in their area to choose retired officers as Area, Zone or Group Organisers. They in turn appointed commanders for each locality.

The success of the LDV in recruiting members alarmed some of the other civil defence organisations, as a resolution placed before Worthing Rural District Council by the local ARP unit shows:

> We view with alarm the probable disintegration of our personnel, which has already commenced, if ex-soldiers leave the ARP service, because naturally they prefer to be classed as soldiers which apparently is possible by joining the Local Defence Volunteers. Sussex Daily News, 22 May 1940

Another organisation found recruitment to the LDV a matter of controversy. Godfrey Wells was a former Canadian Seaforth Highlander, who had fought and been wounded at Vimy Ridge in 1916. He was just the sort of man the LDV were looking for, and he felt that in joining he was 'only exercising the right of any man to defend his hearth and home and those of his neighbours.' However, in the meantime he had become the Vicar of the Subdeanery church at Chichester, and some of his parishioners looked askance at him taking up arms. He was obliged to preach a sermon on the text 'Be strong and of a good courage, for the Lord thy God is with thee,' and ending with the words '"Vengeance is mine, I will repay," saith the Lord.' Revd Wells went on to become the Chaplain to the 1st Sussex Battalion with the rank of Captain. It was later ruled that clergy could enrol in the LDV, but should not be armed, and that sentries using church towers as lookouts should similarly leave their weapons behind (though how far this last injunction was obeyed is open to question).

One further group which took a dim view of the Home Guard was the Germans. On one hand, their broadcasts mocked the idea of all these men being under arms:

> Under what arms? Broomsticks, or the arms of the local pub, with pots of beer and darts in their hands?

and on the other they warned darkly of reprisals against people who, in their view, placed themselves outside international law:

> *Civilians who take up arms against German soldiers are... no better than murderers, whether they are priests or bank clerks.* Quoted in Longmate, Norman, *The Real Dad's Army,* Hutchinson, 1974

At first, the organisers of the LDV were working on a blank canvas. Whereas the Territorial Army Regulations ran to over 500 pages, the rules for setting up the LDV ran to just 29 paragraphs, along with some rather vague letters from the War Office. It was not even clear whether queries about the organisation should be directed to the War Office or the military authorities. This changed radically as the organisation got established. Soon a veritable torrent of paperwork was flowing out to the hapless organisers of local units, covering every conceivable eventuality and oblivious of the fact that the recipients were probably trying to work extended hours in their day job, as well as performing this public service in their spare time. The County Territorial Army Associations were eventually put in charge of their administration: issuing and accounting for all the equipment this new force got, keeping their records and managing their finances (when they finally had some. One thing the Home Guard could not improvise was a budget for their day-to-day

Tank traps of doubtful value. This daunting array outside the Rose and Crown, Tonbridge, seems more likely to trip up passing pedestrians (especially those leaving the pub) than to hold back the German armoured hordes.

Weapons of the Home Guard 4: The Anti-Tank Paintstripper
The No. 68 EY Rifle grenade was an alleged anti-tank weapon, fired from a rifle. It was inaccurate, unreliable (often either going off prematurely or not at all) and ineffective (when tested on a British Matilda tank, it caused severe damage to the paintwork).

running costs, for which the Government had not initially provided. Some units suffered the indignity and inconvenience of having their telephones cut off for non-payment of the bills). Even the TA had to add to their staff to cover the mountain of paperwork involved.

Lieutenant General Sir Cecil Romer, GCB was put in charge of the South-East Region, which took in Kent, all of Sussex and part of Surrey, with its headquarters at Tunbridge Wells. Local headquarters were established at County Hall, Chichester, the Police Station at Lewes and the Territorial Army headquarters in College Road, Maidstone.

Despite the early administrative confusion, the Worthing Home Guard is thought to hold the distinction of being the first in the country to be out on patrol, just twenty-four hours after Eden's broadcast; (some of those on patrol had been Home Guards for less than an hour). At this stage, the Home Guard did not even have identifying armbands, and some of the first patrollers simply tied white handkerchiefs around their arms to indicate some kind of official status. In practice, they probably looked more like the militant wing of a morris-dancing team. As an illustration of the urgency with which the authorities viewed the situation, Eastern Command issued orders for the LDV in Kent and Sussex to have no less than 1,500 armed men on patrol by 18 May, just four days after Eden's speech. Being at the front line of the war, Kent and Sussex had priority for the limited supplies of arms available and were issued with 1,500 rifles and 15,000 rounds of ammunition in time for their first patrol.

The distribution of these weapons did not go entirely smoothly. The rifles were still covered in the grease in which they had been stored, and they had been wrapped for the journey in sacks which had previously been used to transport sand. This was a bad combination for a rifle, and a good deal of cleaning was needed before they would be serviceable. The necessary cleaning equipment had not been supplied and, added to this, many of the men were completely untrained in the use of firearms. Even so, over 1,000 men managed to get out on patrol in Kent alone by 18 May. Most were ex-servicemen, but none had very much idea about what to do in the event of any Germans materialising.

Notwithstanding the early issue of rifles to some of the Kent and Sussex units, weapons were generally in extremely short supply at first. One patrol at Petworth went out in May armed with an old rifle, a shotgun and an otter pole. In Hailsham, the first issue of rifles gave them one, plus ten rounds of ammunition, between fifteen men. They were passed on from patrol to patrol. But even lack of any weapons whatsoever could be overcome by ingenuity. A group of Southern Railway Home Guards in Kent saw a German bomber crash in a newly harvested cornfield near to where they were working. They arrested the pilot, but had no

THESE ARE GERMAN TROOP CARRIERS

JUNKERS JU 52

Dimensions: Span 96 feet, length 62 feet.

Distinguishing features: 1, three engines; 2, low wing; 3, single square cut rudder; 4, sharply tapered wings; 5, square-cut wing tips and tail plane; 6, fixed undercarriage. The most important Nazi troop carrier and the one normally used for parachute dropping.

JUNKERS JU 86

Dimensions: Span 73 feet 8 inches; length 57 feet 4 inches.

Distinguishing features: 1, two engines; 2, low wing; 3, two square cut rudders; 4, sharply tapered wings; 5, square cut wing tips and tail plane; 6, retractable undercarriage.

JUNKERS JU 90

Dimensions: Span 115 feet; length 86 feet.

Distinguishing features: 1, Four engines; 2, low wing; 3, two rudders; 4, tapered wings; 5, leading edge of wing has very pronounced sweep back; 6, square cut wing tips and tail plane; 7, retractable undercarriage.

FOCKE WULF 200 CONDOR

Dimensions: Span 108 feet; length 78 feet.

Distinguishing features: 1, Four engines; 2, low wing; 3, single rudder; 4, tapered wing; 5, rounded wing tips and tail plane; 6, retractable undercarriage; 7, smooth stream-lined fuselage.

These pictures, published at the request of the War Office, are of German troop carriers, and are designed to assist the public to distinguish these machines.

It is suggested that they should be cut out, stuck on cardboard and hung in a prominent place.

Newspapers published these outlines of enemy aircraft as an aid to spotting invaders.

Weapons of the Home Guard 5: Death by Close Support – the Northover Projector

The Northover Projector was designed by a Home Guard officer, a Major H Northover, in the crisis of 1940. It was a cheap (under £10 each) line-of-sight weapon comprising a hollow tube on a tripod. Of 2½-inch calibre, it could fire standard hand or rifle grenades. It also fired SIP grenades, using a toy-pistol cap and a charge of black powder. Whilst SIP grenades were difficult to break when thrown, they were all too inclined to break up in the barrel of a Northover Projector, with most unpleasant effects (especially if the wind was blowing in the line the barrel was pointing). It was also cumbersome to operate, poorly made and prone to breakage, unreliable in damp weather and inaccurate above 150 yards. It also gave off a huge cloud of white smoke, which gave its location away and meant the firers had little chance of getting off a second shot.

But none of these disadvantages could override its major benefit. As Brigadier James Whitehead, London area organiser for the LDV, put it:

'Each of these weapons requires more than one man and if a Northover team consists of three men, they all feel it belongs to them and forget, for the moment at any rate, that they have not got a rifle.' Quoted in Mackenzie, p. 94

Over 8,000 were in use by August 1941. Surprisingly, many Home Guard teams became very attached to these devices. The 19th Kent (Farningham) Battalion of the Home Guard fired green apples from theirs during an exercise in July 1942, and found them 'very effective' at driving off the opposition. One Buckinghamshire platoon developed a 'revolver' version that fired up to twenty grenades a minute.

weapons to detain him until the military arrived. They addressed this by simply confiscating his boots and socks, making it impossible for him to run away over the prickly stubble.

The Margate Home Guard platoon addressed the weapons shortage in a unique way. Their commanding officer, Major Witts, went down to the harbour after the Dunkirk evacuation and found piles of arms and ammunition lying around, abandoned by the returning troops. He quickly requisitioned these and issued them to his 900 men. The authorities heard of this and demanded their return, but he managed to delay doing so under all sorts of pretexts until all the ammunition had been used up and his men had some idea of how to shoot.

Gradually the Home Guard took on a more conventional military appearance, and from August 1940 they were affiliated to their respective county regiments. At first, however, a far looser structure had been envisaged, without even formal rank. Rank itself was a moot matter in the early stages, with some of the officers being more or less self-appointed from among the great and the good of the local community. In the absence of uniforms in the early days, some members would turn up in the uniform in which they had previously served in the regular armed forces. Thus you might find Home Guards with the rank of private but the uniform of a general. One East Sussex company, the House of Commons was told in July 1940, had no less than six generals among its other ranks, all of them wearing their former service uniforms.

Conventional military discipline was problematic in a volunteer force, and there were even cases of squads going on strike against unpopular decisions by the officers. Orders were not infrequently questioned or disregarded and conventional channels for addressing grievances ignored. Weapons were obtained illegally from private sources, or even home-made. Some on the left even saw the units as a prototype People's Militia, no doubt awaiting the opportunity of the glorious revolution. (Given that about 35 per cent of the initial volunteers were ex-servicemen, the prospects of this were remote.)

The newly formed units met wherever they could – schools, church halls, private houses; stranger venues included the county cricket ground at Hove, Goodwood race course, the Connaught Theatre at Worthing and a monastery at Storrington. They improvised both weapons (often more dangerous to themselves than to those at whom they were aimed) and fortifications. Church towers, abandoned cars and mediaeval castles became observation points. In Wilmington, the local Home Guard acquired an old gypsy caravan for this purpose, which they parked on a prominent hilltop and then tried to disguise by painting it in army camouflage colours. Short of fitting it with flashing lights, it would have been hard to make it more obtrusive. In many rural areas, farm carts formed the basis for roadblocks, until some more permanent structure could be manufactured. At Margate, the same function was served by old-fashioned bathing machines filled with sand.

One of their key functions was guarding vital public services and, in many cases, the railway, the utility companies, the Post Office and bus operators set up their own units to guard their own premises. The Short Brothers aircraft factories in Rochester had their own battalion and the 31st Dockyard Battalion became the largest in Kent, with all the several thousand workers at the dockyard eventually becoming eligible for service. Mobile units were also established, using bicycles or, as in the case of Hailsham, half a dozen men piled into the community's taxi cab. A local bus company formed a unit to guard their various depots (originally the Maidstone and District and Allied Companies Battalion, shortened in November 1940

Soldiers practise with a spigot mortar.

> **Weapons of the Home Guard 6: The Bates Eight-Barrel Bottle Thrower**
> This unlikely sounding device was designed to fire a salvo of phosphorous grenades over a distance of a hundred yards. It was eventually rejected on the grounds of being insufficiently manoeuvrable in a mobile war. Even its name was too long.

to the 26th Kent Bus Battalion) but it took until 1943 for someone to realise that a bus battalion would be the ideal nucleus for mobile units. One of the less glamorous tasks was guarding the sewage works, thought to be a prime target for sabotage because of all the public-health problems that would follow from its destruction.

Guard duties could be cold and uncomfortable in these early days, before any decent shelters had been provided. Men would not normally be asked to stand duty for more than half the night, recognising that many of them had day jobs to fill. Gradually, accommodation for the guards was begged, borrowed or improvised – at East Preston, an old beach hut was acquired; while at Charlton, the local sawmill provided the planks to make a rudimentary hut.

But what are they for?
Right from the start, the role of the LDV caused confusion in the highest quarters. Churchill wrote to Anthony Eden on 22 June:

> *Could I have a brief statement of the LDV position, showing the progress achieved in raising and arming them, and whether they are designed for observation or for serious fighting? What is their relationship to the Police, the Military Command and the Regional Commissioners? Who gives them orders and to whom do they report?*

One school of thought was that they might simply employ their local knowledge as look-outs for the regular army (hence another misapplication of their LDV acronym – 'Look, Duck and Vanish'). Wherever possible, men were detailed to patrol in the immediate vicinity of their homes. Others saw the units arresting the hordes of fifth columnists that popular imagination believed were nightly being parachuted into the country. Many innocent people, from courting couples to ornithologists, found themselves arrested for suspicious behaviour, and everything from swans to puffs of smoke from anti-aircraft guns was mistaken for German parachutists. The LDV's role in the event of a full-scale invasion was particularly problematic to many in the regular army, including Ironside. But the idea gradually evolved of them providing static defence in each village, buying time to enable the regular forces to assemble opposition in numbers. In some areas, their duties included blowing up key defensive points that might be of use to an enemy. Crook quotes a member of the Littlehampton platoon:

> *Twice I was rowed across the River Arun, then led through a minefield and thence to a pillbox. Inside was a detonator with instructions to fire it when a code word came in. It would sink a ship down river to block German landing craft and also put the swing bridge out of action. After this, I was expected to fight my way (with an army group nearby) to Arundel a few miles inland.* (Paul Crook. *Sussex Home Guard*, Middleton Press, 1996, p. 28)

By the middle of 1941, the better-armed and trained of the Home Guard units began to be integrated more into the mainstream defence plans of the army (albeit in a role that envisaged them fighting to the last man and round, to buy time for the regular forces. One account tells of a troop who were instructed to fight to the last bullet, then shown how to dismantle their rifles and use them as clubs in hand-to-hand combat.) Some units in the main towns found that they were responsible (possibly with units of the regular army) for a nodal defence point and that, in the event of invasion, their town would become a military strongpoint from which the civilian population would be evacuated, and which would then be expected to hold out for up to a week, before being relieved. Those in the Malling, Tonbridge and Tunbridge Wells battalions found themselves helping to man part of the Ironside Line, a series of pillboxes and tank traps that ran right across Kent and Sussex. In Kent, these followed the River Medway from the Medway towns to beyond Tunbridge Wells.

Some of the more fire-breathing of the local commanders saw their units more as partisan bands, who would roam among the enemy, carrying out hit-and-run attacks and acts of sabotage. This was a bad idea for a number of reasons. First, the army had already set up its own, secret groups to do this (the auxiliary units, discussed later); second, uncontrolled bodies of armed men roaming the countryside were just as likely to confront and attack their own side as the enemy; and third, having an alternative role was likely to cause them to abandon their allotted role of defending their location to the last man. After Ironside gave an inflammatory speech to LDV organisers in June 1940 that left many of them under

This roadblock seems unlikely to delay the panzers for long.

the impression that they had carte blanche to detain, question, beat up or even shoot anyone they wished, instructions had to be issued discouraging some of the wilder ambitions of the force. As a later order put it:

> *The word 'guerrilla' will not be used in future, as it is often misunderstood and if guerrilla activity is generally regarded as a possible secondary role for Home Guard there is a great risk that the obligation to fight to the last in defended localities will not be met.* Southern Command order, June 1942

The training camp for the Home Guard, set up as a private initiative in the grounds of Osterley Park, the home of the Earl of Jersey, may have helped to fuel the ambitions for guerrilla war. A variety of instructors, several of them veterans of the Spanish Civil War, taught the arts of 'ungentlemanly combat'. The enterprise was heavily publicised in *Picture Post* (whose proprietor, Edward Hulton, was one of the champions of the scheme) and was a huge success. (Many of the staff at the school were later investigated by MI5, as having what MI5 saw as suspiciously left-wing sympathies.) A similar school was established at Bowmans Farm, Burwash by Major John Langdon-Davies, a former journalist who had covered the Spanish Civil War for the *News Chronicle*. As with Osterley Park, this camp was at first not officially recognised, and was paid for by the *Sunday Pictorial*. They taught Home Guard members every aspect of guerrilla warfare, to a sufficiently high standard for the school to receive official recognition by South-Eastern Command. A reporter from the *Sussex Daily News* visited in late 1941:

> *From the moment they* [the Home Guards attending the course] *enter the farm gates from a twisting muddy lane they consider themselves to be under fire from a nearby village* [Burwash] *and in the presence of a more or less firmly established enemy. Hence every single thing they do for three nights and two days is done with the feeling at the back of the mind of every individual – a feeling*

Weapons of the Home Guard 7: Big Boys' Toys

The Smith Gun, first delivered in 1942, was the brainchild of a toy manufacturer. It was a 3-inch smooth-bored gun on a simple two-wheeled trailer that could be towed by any car (though its unsprung wheels were not designed for this purpose). In combat, the gun was turned on its side. Using one of the wheels as its base, it could then traverse instantly through 360 degrees. Recoil from the gun was dealt with by a system of rubber bands. It fired high-explosive and hollow-charge bombs, and could potentially have done serious damage to a tank, penetrating 80mm of armour at 50 yards. However, it was variously described by its operators as 'a brute of a weapon' and as having 'a terrifying record for killing its crews'. It was also inaccurate, heavy and awkward to use and had an effective range of just 100 to 300 yards. The authorities nonetheless gave its introduction much publicity and some of its operators (those who survived) even grew fond of it. Some 3,000 were in use by early 1943. One thing that minimised its destructive capabilities for all concerned was that shortage of ammunition meant users rarely had more than six or seven rounds per gun.

Home Guards at a Town Fighting School 'somewhere in England' demonstrate the art of chasing 'Jerry' across a toggle rope bridge.

> *which is encouraged – that somewhere among those not so distant beeches or clumps of bracken an enemy is crouched to kill; and the task is under those very eyes to learn how to outwit him.* Quoted in Crook, pp. 38-9

The first night, they had the relative comfort of a barn to sleep in. Thereafter they were bivouacking under hedges. They learned camouflage, stalking, unarmed combat and living off the land, along with weapons skills. Around 3,000 Home Guards were put through this tough finishing school. The *Sussex Daily News* reporter picked up on the ungentlemanly nature of it all: 'One came away deeply impressed with the purpose of it all; in short to combine the attributes of the gamekeeper and the guttersnipe.' Another such school was set up in Amberley, West Sussex, and Eastbourne (and later, Worthing) had a Town Fighting School, teaching the principles of house-to-house fighting in urban areas in a derelict residential area at the eastern end of the town.

For those not selected for these training courses, exercises provided the best opportunity of experiencing something approaching battlefield conditions. Some of these were valuable in exposing gaps in local defences (such as the Eastbourne Battalion's successful attack on the Wish Tower in February 1942). After Lieutenant General Bernard Montgomery took over South-Eastern Command in November 1941, the tempo of these was greatly increased, as he tried to bring the Home Guard nearer to the standard of the regular troops. Regular Canadian troops, based at Goring-by-Sea, were bought in to train the Home Guard in street-fighting, unarmed combat, night patrols and other skills, some of the exercises using live ammunition. Montgomery praised the 'mutual respect and comradeship' that had been developed during the course of these exercises, and thought they would 'prove of the greatest value should we be called upon to defeat an attempted invasion of our country.' On occasions, their local knowledge could put them at a real advantage against their opponents. In one exercise, the Sheppey Battalion found their regular army opponents barricaded inside a glass factory in Queenborough. They were able to gain entry through an underground duct known only to the locals and take them by complete surprise.

By the end of September 1940, almost half the Home Guard were still not armed – they were 740,000 weapons short. A not entirely satisfactory solution to the problem was achieved by the Government obtaining a large supply of Canadian Ross and American Springfield, Remington and Eddystone rifles. The Ross had been withdrawn during the First World War on account of their tendency to jam, and they all had spent the last twenty years stored in a thick grease (which made their preparation for use an unpleasant process). They also fired .300 ammunition, which nothing else in the British Army used and for which there was no British manufacturing facility. Supplies of ammunition were consequently very short (about fifty rounds apiece, doled out in handfuls). Many Home Guards were consequently unpractised in the use of firearms in the early stages. The .300 rifles all had a red band painted on them, to stop the user loading standard .303 ammunition. This could be loaded, but if fired tended to jam in the breech and cause the barrel to blow up.

Rifle ranges were gradually set up as ammunition became available to practise with. Some units even built their own ranges, like the one in the Heathfield Park sandstone quarry. The training given to men before letting them loose on the ranges could, to put it mildly, be variable. A member of the East Marden Unit recalls being handed a Browning automatic rifle, helping to degrease it and then being given a bandolier of ammunition and told to go and fire it on the range, as a means of finding out how it worked. Accidents were not unknown.

Home Guard communications varied from the primitive (boys on bicycles and men on roller-skates carrying messages) to state of the art. Brighton Home Guards had their own private telephone lines laid, in case the public ones were destroyed, and other units had army-specification portable radios, and personnel trained at the Post Office Signals School at Brighton.

Various specialised units were formed. In Worthing, a Naval Observation Post was set up, to give some of the more elderly ex-naval recruits a chance to serve in a more sedentary role. Decontamination squads were formed in many of the coastal towns, such as Eastbourne and Hastings. Rivers had floating patrols of converted pleasure boats and as many as 900 Home Guards nationwide served in cavalry units, patrolling the moors, downs and coastlines. In particular, the 'Lewes Cossacks' attracted up to fifty members and a good deal of press interest, not least since two of its members (riders, rather than horses) were former Grand National winners. Many of the units did excellent civil defence work, dealing with the aftermath of the heavy bombing that many towns suffered. There were even Home Guard military bands, though their contribution to the nation's security remains a matter of speculation.

One of the duties of the LDV was to examine the identity cards of those they met on their patrols or on the multitude of roadblocks they manned. The roadblocks in particular were a cause of delay, which provoked local road-users' resentment; there were 625 of them in the Medway towns alone. Some were built so tightly that not even normal traffic could get through them. One such, erected on a bridge at Margate, closed it to all traffic for a full day until it could be widened.

Some people failed to stop at them, either deliberately, or because they did not see the poorly lit obstacle. In some cases, this led to the unhappy victim being shot. In Eastbourne, Crook tells the story of a cyclist who, when challenged, would persist in shouting: 'I'm no bloody Jerry. I don't stop for you!' and riding straight through the men on guard. He was cured of this one night by one of the patrol jamming his rifle butt into the spokes of his front wheel, sending him over the handlebars. The soldier then stood over the bloodied figure with his rifle pointed in his face, cocked it and said: 'When we say halt, what we really mean is "Bloody Well HALT!"' The man never did it again.

Nobody was too grand or too humble to be detained by a roadblock. The Sheppey Battalion opened fire on a car which failed to stop, only to discover that they had come close to shooting the Mayoress, returning from an official engagement. One Home Guard patrol even detained a suspicious-looking black car with its number plate missing. They demanded to see the identity papers of the occupants, until the window was wound down and he was introduced as King George VI. At the other extreme, a Hastings woman took exception to one of these barriers after a night of heavy drinking, and set about the unequal task of trying to

Substantial road barriers in Tonbridge High Street.

Weapons of the Home Guard 8: The Blacker Bombard, or spigot mortar

This was the brainchild of Lieutenant Colonel L V S Blacker, and was another reject from the regular army (who had turned it down in favour of the 2-inch mortar in 1939). He revamped it as a combined anti-tank and bombardment weapon, sold it successfully to Winston Churchill (if not his military advisors) and it began to appear towards the end of 1941. It again had its flaws – it was inaccurate (General de Gaulle was almost killed by it at its first demonstration, which may have further endeared it to Churchill), heavy, immobile, and desperately slow to fire. The ammunition supplied for it was also badly fused, and a shell could pass right through an unarmoured vehicle without exploding. It came in a mobile version, with legs, or could be fired off a fixed concrete pedestal in a defensive position. It fired finned bombs and had an effective range of 75-200 yards.

But it was even better than the Northover Projector, in the sense that it could absorb the attentions of a five-man Home Guard crew (without rifles). Much public-relations effort was expended on showing that the Home Guard with the Blacker Bombard was a serious fighting force. It was also known by the less medieval (and more prosaic) name of the Spigot Mortar. About 18,000 were in use by early 1943.

demolish it with a hacksaw. She was rapidly arrested and, after repeating her attempted demolition act on a police cell, received a month's hard labour.

The force gradually started to become more mobile. As we have heard, some of the younger and fitter Home Guards were equipped with bicycles or cars, so that they might go out to deal with any reports of parachutists dropping within a few miles of their base. Specified petrol stations were earmarked for the use of Home Guard vehicles, in the event of invasion. In this event, areas like Eastbourne and Hailsham could turn out a thousand or so fully equipped Home Guards, ready for action, within ninety minutes. Getting the Home Guard units up as near as possible to the standard of the regular forces also came to have a propaganda, as well as a practical, purpose, since it enabled the Government to present the Home Guard as a hardened force, capable of taking over home defence and freeing the regular army for a (dummy) invasion in 1943. From the start of 1941, fears of invasion had started to recede and complacency began to set in. A report to the Chiefs of Staff in January 1941 confirmed that 'there was little doubt that the public were taking the whole thing much more casually than they had last summer.' The number of Home Guards began to decline – by about 150,000 nationally in the last six months of 1941 – and this left some units in the south-east particularly short of manpower to perform their duties. (Members could leave the force with two weeks' notice on either side – the so-called 'Maid's clause'.) The matter became a scandal when it was reported that some German airmen who had baled out had found difficulty in getting anyone to arrest them! This complacency was not shared by General (later Field Marshal Lord) Alan Brooke or Churchill, who believed that the Russian campaign would offer no more than a few months' respite from the threat of invasion. There were also those among the general public who were convinced that things had gone quiet because Hitler was digging the first Channel Tunnel! The introduction of conscription in December 1941, under which all males aged between eighteen and fifty-one were liable to be called up for the Home Guard, did much to reduce the decline in membership of the force, which was particularly marked in the south-east.

One further area of diversification was into anti-aircraft duties. From September 1941, regular troops began to be moved out of Anti-Aircraft Command and were replaced with Home Guards – about 11,000 had trained as gunners by May 1942, and a year later the total rose to 111,917. They also undertook bomb disposal and civil defence work. As the immediate threat of invasion receded, Home Guard units were also able to release regular soldiers of the Royal Artillery manning coastal batteries overlooking the Channel for other duties. They received thirty-six hours of training over a four-week period before being unleashed on what was still the front part of Britain's front line. On one of the ex-naval guns at Aldwick, the range-finding and other instructions to the gun crew were given by a fifteen-year-old boy.

Despite the gourmet promise of being able to dine off army rations while on duty, some areas found it difficult to attract enough volunteers for coastal defence duties. Special recruiting drives were held and, in West Sussex in 1943, commanding officers were given the power to transfer men compulsorily onto

The Royal Observer Corps was one of the many areas where women contributed to the war effort.

these duties. They even went as far as designating the Home Guards manning coastal defences as key personnel, and held out the possibility of such troops having their call-up to the regular army deferred, should it come. The units even got to man some of the bigger artillery – the 6-inch naval guns at the Wish Tower at Eastbourne and batteries of a similar calibre at Bexhill both came under Home Guard control in 1942. In this case, three months' training was deemed necessary.

Auxiliary units

I have been following with much interest the growth and development of the new guerrilla formations... known as 'Auxiliary Units'. From what I hear these units are being organised with thoroughness and imagination, and should, in the event of invasion, prove a useful addition to the regular forces. Perhaps you will keep me informed of progress. Winston Churchill to the Secretary of State for War, 25 September 1940

These anonymously named units of the Home Guard were, in fact, the nearest thing the British forces had to suicide squads. The idea originated from General Andrew Thorne, who was in charge of XII Corps and responsible for the defence of Kent, Sussex and part of Surrey. The conventional resources at his disposal were limited:

Its strength in early June was made up largely of one Territorial division, one theoretically motorised brigade, 5,000 stevedores armed with rifles, a District Headquarters and a miscellany of minor units; there was little artillery, hardly any ammunition, and the standard of training was low. The Corps was responsible for a front extending from Greenwich to Hayling Island, and its commander had no illusions about his ability to drive back into the sea, or even to contain, strong German forces if they succeeded in getting ashore. Peter Fleming. Operation Sea Lion, Pan, 1975, p. 269

The defensive plan was that his regular force, if driven back from the coast, would stand and fight at General Headquarters (GHQ) line, a hastily improvised defensive line around the southern outskirts of London. As the invasion force made its way inland, the auxiliary units, small teams of selected Home Guard members under the control of a specially trained army officer, would emerge from hiding and do what they could to disrupt the progress of the enemy until they were killed or could rejoin the Allied lines. The authorities gave them a life expectancy of just two weeks. Although the idea originated in Kent, other commanders adopted it in various parts of the country. Overall responsibility for setting these groups up nationwide was given to Colonel Colin Gubbins.

The model for these units was Section D, part of the pre-war Secret Intelligence Service, whose task was to 'investigate every possibility of attacking potential enemies by means other than the operations of military forces.' Most of their work was carried out overseas, but one unit which remained operational throughout the war was based in the Star Brewery, Eastbourne, and was manned by four of the people working there, including one of its owners. They had stores of explosives, weapons and radio equipment hidden in the top of the brewery's water tower.

Weapons of the Home Guard 9: Medieval close support – the Pike

Here lies a victim of them Huns;
He had a pike and they had guns.
But now he wonders, gone aloft,
Whether to blame the Huns or Croft*.

Daily Mail, February 1942

Perhaps the most ill-advised armament decision of the war was the War Office order, placed in July 1941, for 250,000 pikes – scaffolding poles with army-surplus bayonets welded on the end. Churchill, recognising the shortage of weapons, had argued for this, on the grounds that 'a man thus armed may easily acquire a rifle for himself'. It was seen as a death wish by those who saw that they may have to face panzers with such weapons, and as class warfare by those who regarded their use in the square-bashing aspects of the service as imposing the will of the capitalist ruling elite. Among the public the proposal excited ridicule, in the Home Guard outrage. Lord Croft*, the junior War Minister who took the blame for the decision, was depicted in newspaper cartoons wearing full armour, and sarcastic editorials speculated on what other medieval instruments of warfare might be introduced. There were angry exchanges on the matter in both Houses of Parliament, and many consignments were delivered straight into storage, to avoid demoralising the men.

Around 20 of these units were created nationally at first but, by late 1941, there were 21 in Sussex and 33 in Kent, totalling some 342 men. Each consisted of an officer and his 'striking force' of up to 12 soldiers, in some cases supplemented by signallers, a clerk and a storeman. They had limited links in the surrounding area to Home Guard members, and to Scout patrols within the regular army. They were:

> *...selected for their resourcefulness, their knowledge of the country and their skill in high explosives. These men were trained, mostly at the weekends, in sabotage and the use of high explosive; and as the dumps and hideaways began to be established they assumed responsibility for them.* Fleming, p. 271. Peter Fleming, the originator of this part of the war effort, was also the author of *Operation Sea Lion*, which was a source for this book. His indirect claim to fame is as the brother of James Bond creator, Ian Fleming.)

A E Cocks describes his introduction to the force. He was invited to the local schoolmaster's house and told of plans to create an underground resistance movement – a form of Commando, except they would not be a uniformed part of the British Army. He was told that he had been recommended by his commanding officer in the Home Guard 'and by other sources', and had been vetted by the Chief Constable. As part of his training, he would have to get to know every inch of the land within five miles of his home. He agreed to join and was asked to sign the Official Secrets Act. Everything about them was highly secretive – their training manual was designed to look, to the casual observer, like a countryman's diary, and not even their families could be told about their role. According to Kieser, one

Weapons of the Home Guard 10: The Sten Gun
Designed in 1940 by two officers named Shepherd and Turpin (the ST of the name – the EN is for Enfield, the Royal Small Arms Factory which manufactured it), it was an automatic gun, firing a 32-shot magazine of standard 9mm ammunition at around 500 shots per minute. Very simple and cheap to make (under £1.75, by some accounts), millions were produced, and were used by regular forces, overseas Resistance groups and by the Home Guard. Around 248,000 were in use by the Home Guard by the start of 1943 and 40 per cent of the Home Guard were eventually issued with these, in lieu of rifles.

wife went for years under the illusion that her husband was having an affair, due to his frequent, lengthy and unexplained absences.

Their training consisted of learning to use a wide range of weapons, unarmed combat and techniques for avoiding detection, from how to move silently across country at night to standing still for extended periods. Regular exercises were arranged, consisting mostly, it seemed, of making life a misery for the regular Canadian troops stationed in the area. The Ashburnham and Crowhurst patrols breached security at Battle Abbey, taking the Canadian commanding officer prisoner and disabling all their vehicles. The irate Canadians thought the regular local Home Guard were responsible, went round to the pub they frequented and beat them up. The Bishopstone patrol actually placed a small explosive charge under the seat of their local Canadian CO, which he detonated by sitting down. Ringmer patrol terrorised an entire hall full of Canadians at Brighton, by removing slates from the roof and dropping thunder-flashes among them. Many other cases of less spectacular breaches of their security exist, but the Canadians had their occasional moments of revenge, such as when they discovered the headquarters of the Firle patrol and ransacked it. Other auxiliary units breached the security of the area's radar stations.

Had the invasion taken place, the first of these units called into action would have been those of XII Corps. They were officially known as the 203rd Battalion of the Home Guard, and covered the area from Kent to Cornwall. (The others were the 201st, covering Scotland, and the 202nd for northern England). Since they were not officially recognised as part of the regular British armed forces, had they been brought into action and caught, they would have been denied the protection of the Geneva Convention and shot.

One of their first jobs would have been to blow up any bridges and buildings that might be of use to the enemy. Some of these structures were wired up for instant detonation, and not all the wiring was removed at the end of the war. One bridge near Margate was found to be still ready to blow at a moment's notice in 1978. Other units were responsible for different kinds of chaos. The Iden patrol would have been disrupting traffic on the railway line at Rye and the A259 and A268 roads to Ashford and London leading out of the town. The post-invasion task of the Ditchling patrol was to destroy the underground petrol tanks at Chailey airfield. Wiston had the job of triggering a series of flame fougasses on the road into Steyning. Other units surveyed the layouts and grounds of the main stately homes in their areas, on the assumption that the Germans would occupy these as headquarters buildings and they would need to infiltrate them.

Gulvin tells the story of General Montgomery gaining first-hand experience of the units' skills at concealment in 1941:

> *Captain Fleming took the General for a walk along the top of Charing Hill and at the Captain's invitation they sat down on an old trough to admire the view. After several minutes the General looked round and found that the Captain had gone. This was most puzzling as there was apparently nowhere to hide and he had not been gone long enough to get out of sight. Then suddenly Captain Fleming's voice came up from below the trough. The General looked down to see Captain Fleming's head appear out of an opening in the bottom of the old trough.* K R Gulvin. *The Kent Home Guard*, North Kent Books, 1980, p. 87

Their subterranean bases took a variety of forms. One was in the disused cellars of an abandoned house; another enlarged the tunnels of a badgers' sett in a derelict chalk-pit; a third – the largest, able to house up to 120 men – was located beneath an oval pit at Godmersham Park, near Bilting, dug during the First World War to house an airship. The smallest was the two-man observation post described above. Others were effectively Nissen huts, buried in the ground by Royal Engineers. Old smugglers' caves and tunnels were also brought back into use; one such led into the heart of RAF Manston, and could have been ideal for infiltration, in the event that the Germans had taken the airfield over. This was eventually destroyed by one of the air raids on Manston. They concentrated on providing the essentials for a guerrilla campaign, rather than any concession to domestic luxury, as this description of the Icklesham base illustrates:

> *Our 'hideout' or 'O.B.' was in a wood by a sandpit – down the road before the Robin Hood, from Icklesham to Pett. The Royal Engineers built it, as we worked such long hours on the farms. It was made from corrugated iron and timber and was 15 feet by 10 feet, and just over six feet high. The entrance was through a hatch, counterbalanced, which was covered with twigs and leaves. We then went down a shaft by a wooden ladder. There was a 15 feet long wooden emergency tunnel exit to the edge of the sandpit. Inside the hideaway were triple bunks, food for about three weeks, water in milk churns, ammunition, explosives, a small stove for cooking and a chemical toilet.* Colin Cooke, quoted in Josephine Kirkham (ed), *Rye's War*, Rye Museum Association, 2002, pp. 12-13

Cooke explained the role of his unit:

> *We were not supposed to stand up and fight, there were only six of us, but we were meant to slow the Germans down, with things like trip wires attached to explosives and 'flesh cutters'. We were to sabotage what we could. The Army taught us shooting and we could have done quite a lot of damage by blowing up munitions, bridges, railway lines and such like. We aimed to patrol at night and to snipe at them. We were also meant to get information back [to the Resistance HQ].* Kirkham, p. 13

> **Weapons of the Home Guard 11: The Fougasse**
> This consisted of a large oil drum, set into the bank alongside a sunken road. It was filled with a mixture of petrol and tar which, when detonated, would cover anything near it in a ball of flame and smoke. It was detonated by an SIP grenade, fixed to the drum and let off by pulling a cord. Later versions had electric detonators, and multiple fougasses could be set up, often to reinforce roadblocks.

Like their conventional Home Guard counterparts, the auxiliary units supplemented their ordinary armaments with improvised weapons. One unit used to remove the No. 5 shot from twelve-bore cartridges, which in their estimation would not stop anything larger than rabbits, and half-fill the resultant cavity with boiling mutton fat (not a job for the faint-hearted). This was said to congeal into a plug that would penetrate corrugated iron at 25 yards. This was possibly a more practical option than the official War Department approach to making shotguns more lethal – a shotgun cartridge firing a single solid ball, which very quickly wore away the barrel of the shotgun.

Jack Matthews, the leader of Iden Patrol, described their equipment in more detail:

> *Our hideout (O.B.) was in Norland Wood, 500 yards east of Peasmarsh Church... We had scores of grenades and spare detonators; hurricane lamps; picks and shovels; numerous rolls each of tripwire and trapwire (they were different!); a lot of pull and release switches; all kinds of ammunition; 10 gallons of paraffin; a large amount of plastic high explosive; many one-hour and three-hour delay switches for booby traps; lots of striker boards and magnets; hundreds of time pencils; sticky bombs to put on armoured vehicles and black, brown and green camouflage colours to put on our hands and faces. Each of us had a small, very sharp, hook shaped knife to cut tyres. The first aid kits had morphine to use as a painkiller, or in a large dose, for suicide. There was also a gallon jar of rum!* Jack Matthews, quoted in Kirkham, p. 16

In addition to these stores, units might have stocks of gelignite buried in the woods nearby. They were often buried in fox-or rabbit-holes, since the animals were known to choose dry banks for their homes. Stored under the wrong conditions, these caches could become unstable. A number were found after the war, and had to be dealt with by bomb-disposal experts. One member of the Small Dole patrol, George Cooper, took his work home with him and neglected to deal with the supplies of ammunition and explosives buried in his garden during his lifetime. This provided an entirely unexpected garden feature for the people who bought his house when he died. In similar vein, the purchasers of a Kent house in the 1980s discovered that their loft insulation consisted largely of a supply of elderly Molotov cocktails.

The headquarters of the auxiliary units was at Coleshill House, at Highworth near Swindon, where they were taught unarmed combat, night scouting (they would wear welders' goggles to get used to working in the dark) and the use of explosives. The Sussex base of the 203rd Battalion was at Tottington Manor at

A flame fougasse in action, in a trial in a sandpit near Erith. Here at least was one Home Guard weapon that might gain the undivided attention of a German panzer.

Small Dole, West Sussex. Two Scout patrols of regular soldiers were attached to Tottington, to assist in the training of all the local auxiliary units. Fleming himself had his base at The Garth at Bilting, a country house on the road between Ashford and Canterbury. This also became something of a training centre, where each weekend some fifty to eighty men gradually became proficient in weapons new (plastic explosive) and old (the longbow). The latter, at least, could be practised in public whilst the former also proved to be a very effective way of catching fish at Tottington Manor. The auxiliary units tended to get access to the latest weaponry well before it was available to the regular army.

In addition to many of the improvised weapons available to the Home Guard (and described elsewhere) the auxiliary units had access to a range of booby-trap devices: pressure switches, to detonate an explosion when pushed down; their opposite, the release switch, which detonates when pressure is released (say, by lifting a trapdoor); tripwires that could set off charges, and the Anti-Personnel Switch, which fired a bullet through the foot of anyone stepping on it (and, with any luck, into other parts of them as well). They were also shown how to improvise simple but effective booby traps: the hand grenade, disguised to look like a piece of coal and left in the fireside bucket, and the romantic candle in a bottle that was actually a bomb.

As the D-Day invasion of Normandy grew nearer, members of various patrols were approached with a view to dropping into occupied territory before the invasion and causing various kinds of havoc. This ill-considered scheme disregarded the fact that the auxiliary units depended upon having intimate knowledge of their locality. Any advantage they had would be lost, blundering round a piece of foreign countryside by night. The idea was apparently dropped on the insistence of the Pensions Department, who foresaw all sorts of difficult claims from the dependants of volunteers dropped over foreign territory and later killed.

Had they gone into action, the units would have operated under a number of handicaps. Although they were vetted by the head of the local police force, the rank-and-file police knew nothing of their existence and could have become awkward if they were found out at night without any good reason that they could reveal. There was also no communication between the groups – in the interests of security they were kept in ignorance of neighbouring units. This would, however, have made co-ordinated action by them impossible and may have limited their potential impact. As soon as they started causing any problems, tracker dogs would have been bought in, and it would only have been a matter of time before their base camps were found. Food supplies would have run out within two weeks and the need to live off the land thereafter would have further increased their risk of capture. Last, and by no means least, there was the likelihood that the occupying forces would have taken severe reprisals against the communities in which the units were operating, which again would have opened them to the danger of betrayal. The auxiliary units were denied the cyanide pills that were made available to the Special Operations Executive, but their medical kit included enough morphine to make a fatal dose, should circumstances have demanded it.

Rarely can the British genius for improvisation have been put to such good effect as in the setting up of the Home Guard. But, for all their numbers, they could never have been more than a helpful adjunct to the mainstream forces. Once the initial trauma of Dunkirk was over, how did the island's defences as a whole look?

Chapter Four

A very good anti-tank obstacle

The more I see of conditions at home the more bewildered I am as to what has been going on in this country since the war started! It is now ten months and yet the shortage of trained men and of equipment is appalling!! At present I fail to see how we can make this country safe against attack. Alex Danchev and Daniel Todman (eds). *War Diaries 1939-1945*, Field Marshall Lord Alanbrooke, (Weidenfeld and Nicholson, 2001), 1 July 1940

At any rate I must admit you have a very good anti-tank obstacle. French general Maxime Weygand to Winston Churchill (referring to the English Channel), June 1940

Julius Caesar: early plans against invasion

Invasion does not appear to have been on the agenda for British military planning before the war. Captain Basil Liddell Hart, who was not only a military correspondent to the *Telegraph* and *The Times*, but was also until 1938 personal advisor to the Secretary of State for War, wrote in July 1939:

England... is... more secure than ever before against invasion... There is sound cause for discounting the danger of invasion... The development of air power has greatly diminished the possibility of sea-borne invasion. A landing on a foreign coast has always been the most difficult operation of war. It has now become much more difficult, indeed almost impossible. Basil Liddell Hart. *The Defence of Britain*, Faber and Faber, 1939

During the First World War, even in times of grave manpower shortage, a division (generally of the regular army) had been kept at home, partly against the threat of civil disorder in Ireland or elsewhere, but also to guard against the possible invasion of the British east coast. But by 1939, the view that 'the bombers will always get through' may have made bombing look like a more risk-free option than invasion for an enemy looking to bring a nation to its knees.

As the possibility of invasion began to register, the Chiefs of Staff commissioned some initial investigations of possible anti-invasion measures. The plan for dealing with an invasion, which emerged between October 1939 and the spring of 1940, was called *Julius Caesar*. Its basic assumptions were that the capture of a port, made possible largely by landing German paratroops, would be followed by the landing of sea-borne troops in large numbers. It made some serious overestimates of the German capacity to mount the initial sea-borne attack and equally underestimated the logistical difficulties of doing so.

The plan's response to this threat was to capture or destroy the airborne troops before they could capture a port. It was based upon a number of more or less questionable assumptions; first, that a combination of sea-power, the air force and coastal defences would prevent most of the invaders from getting ashore. Second,

DUNLOP TYRES do their Duty

40H/122

War is good business... Just as modern tyre manufacturers use grand prix cars to glamorise their products, so images of war sold tyres in the 1940s.

that even the weakened divisions available to the home forces were sufficient, both to arrest the paratroops before they could fulfil their function and to neutralise those few sea-borne troops that did manage to get ashore. Early experience of protecting the British fleet from German bombers and submarines did not inspire confidence in the first of these assumptions. The second was wholly untested.

In the event that a serious German invasion did make progress, there were also contingency plans for the country to be divided into twelve regions, each run by a commissioner with the powers to co-ordinate local services independent of Central Government, should communications between the two break down. The War Cabinet would move to near Worcester, Parliament to Stratford-upon-Avon, while each of the service ministries would also relocate – the Admiralty to Malvern, the War Office to Droitwich and the Air Ministry to Worcester.

At that time, the idea of combined operations between the forces was not a well-developed one (on either side), and the defensive proposals which emerged were correspondingly fragmented. The plan involved the setting up of some mobile forces to deal with smaller landings, but had no real arrangements for combining reconnaissance with offensive action against the invader. The number of troops available and their training in mobile warfare was also wholly inadequate for the task.

In public, General Ironside talked up the strength of the army. This was how he portrayed the situation shortly before the German onslaught in the west:

> *I tremble to think what might have happened if we had been attacked during the first months of the war. We had then no army at all, whereas now we have a very fine army. Thank goodness Hitler missed the bus. He did not take the opportunity which was the one thing we feared more than anything. We have now actually turned the corner.* General Ironside, quoted in *Sussex Daily News*, 3 April 1940

The accuracy of his assessment can be judged from chapter 2. As France's defeat began to take on a horrible inevitability, the Chiefs of Staff reviewed the domestic situation. They concluded on 22 May that:

> *The whole crux of the problem is the air defence of this country...* [The country must be] *organised as a fortress on totalitarian lines.* Basil Collier. *The Defence of the United Kingdom*, HMSO, 1957, p. 119

That same day, the Government took on those totalitarian powers, through the Emergency Powers (Defence) Act. Ironside took over command of the home forces just as the withdrawal from Dunkirk began. He had to carry out a swift and radical reassessment of the plans for home defence. They lacked manpower and resources, they lacked transport, and their tactics had been shown by events in France to be seriously inadequate. As at the end of May 1940 Ironside had fifteen infantry divisions at home, most of them at half-strength or less, and an incomplete 2nd Armoured Division.

Ironside's key objective in his new plan was to put enough force in depth up against the Germans before they could reach London or the industrial heartlands of the Midlands and the North. He identified the GHQ line, referred to earlier; a fortified line to which his forces would fall back if initial lines of defence failed. This ran south from The Wash, through Cambridge and around London, as far

The 3.7-inch anti-aircraft gun was gradually being introduced as war started.

south as Maidstone. It then turned west towards Basingstoke, then north to the Reading area and westwards to Bristol. In front of that, three advance stop lines ran through Surrey, Sussex and Kent, with others covering the approaches from East Anglia. These lines of static defence were designed to confine and delay the enemy until better-equipped help could arrive. Where possible, these used natural obstacles like watercourses, railway embankments and steep hills to increase their delaying power.

But his troops were not only inexperienced and ill-equipped. They were also fatally immobile, given that Ironside was defending almost 500 miles of coastline against invasion, as well as facing the possibility of airborne troops landing almost anywhere inland. The troops' supplies had transport but, if the soldiers themselves had to travel beyond walking distance, they were forced to rely upon hired coaches and buses and their civilian drivers. Eight or even as much as twenty-four hours' notice might be required to get the defending forces on a mobile footing in numbers. This meant that even small armoured landing forces could have made considerable progress inland before encountering any substantial opposition. On a visit to the 3rd Division in July 1940, Churchill was dismayed to find that, while they lacked any vehicles to patrol the 30 miles of coastline for which they were responsible, there were still buses plying for pleasure trips along the nearby Brighton seafront.

Equally risky was the fact that such a large part of the home forces was committed to coastal defence – eight of his fifteen infantry divisions were so employed, with much of the rest deployed with a view to rounding up airborne troops to their rear. Just three divisions were held back at GHQ Reserve, which was stationed on a line running between Northampton, London and Aldershot, with the 2nd Armoured Division based in Lincolnshire. Only the most exposed parts of the coastline, between The Wash and Sussex, could claim to be even moderately well protected. Here, Eastern Command had six infantry divisions, albeit with about half the field artillery and a fraction of the anti-tank weapons they needed. The 1st London Division, covering the area between Sheppey and Rye, had twenty-three of its establishment of seventy-two field guns, no anti-tank guns, no armoured cars or tanks, no medium machine guns and a sixth of the anti-tank rifles they needed.

The Chiefs of Staff were under no illusions about their ability to withstand invasion. They estimated that fewer than 5,000 parachute troops could have taken over seven key airfields for long enough to allow Luftwaffe bombers free rein and to get up to 20,000 troops, supported by armour, ashore. The fixed defences were weak and the seizure of airfields would deprive Britain of vital early warning from air reconnaissance.

> *Should the Germans succeed in establishing a force with its vehicles in this country, our armed forces have not got the offensive power to drive it out.* Chiefs of Staff, quoted in Collier, p. 125

Most of their field guns were stationed near the most likely landing places, but the majority of anti-tank weapons remained with the reserves in GHQ. Beaches were mined and obstructed, inland roads were blocked (something that would have proved as much of a hindrance to the movement of our troops and emergency services as it would to any would-be invader), and stocks of incendiary weapons

St Martin's Battery was built on top of Victorian gun emplacements, overlooking the harbour at Dover. The 1940s emplacements, but not the guns, survive.

and sticky bombs were supplied to each guard post. Home Guard patrols manned roadblocks and there were some cases where either motorists failed to slow down in good time (possibly because roadblocks were difficult to spot in the blackout) or the Home Guards became trigger-happy, or both, and a small number of motorists were killed. The German propaganda machine seized on this and their account of events soon put the death-toll from this cause at more than 400. Pillboxes and tank traps were erected along the stop lines. Defence against aerial troops landing also became a preoccupation. Strange wigwam-like obstacles were erected above straight lengths of road and assorted obstructions were placed in open fields to deter landings by glider.

By the second half of June, some 150,000 people, military and civilian, were working feverishly to put the physical infrastructure of the new defence plans in place. Churchill was concerned that so many military personnel were being tied up by these fortification works. He claimed that only 57,000 civilian workers were being used. However, the use of civilian contractors without proper military supervision inevitably led to blunders. There were roadblocks that armoured vehicles could simply drive round and others that even civilian vehicles could not get through; pillboxes that faced the wrong way, or were simply in the wrong place, serving no conceivable military purpose.

The plan was also ill-conceived in military terms. The need to garrison so many static lines and defensive points left too few troops to mount an effective counter-attack. Those troops that were available for countermeasures could not be mobilised quickly enough and, with little armour or transport, their offensive capability was limited. The net result of this was that any German invaders faced only a thin crust of defence on the coast, with no major opposition until they had had an opportunity to make serious progress inland. General Ironside's tenure as head of the home forces was to be a short one.

Under new management

By early September 1940, the home forces had recovered a little from the desperate condition they had been in after Dunkirk, but they were still far from strong. There were only about four fully equipped divisions and a further eight reasonably well equipped. The rest lacked key equipment, especially transport. About half the infantry divisions had had little training. There were now some good mobile troops, but they were inexperienced in dealing with German blitzkrieg tactics and there was little experience of joint army/air force operations. At least the Home Guard was not in short supply. They now numbered almost half a million, with their younger members forming mobile units with cars, cycles and motorcycles.

But, more important, there was a new man in charge. General Ironside had been replaced as head of the home forces in July 1940 by General Alan Brooke, who had made his name managing the retreat of the British Expeditionary Force in France. He was much more committed to a more mobile and aggressive form of warfare, in line with Churchill's thinking. In the following sections, we look at what, under Brooke's command, would have confronted any German invading force.

The watery front line

Britain's front line started beyond our shores. The responsibility for stopping an invasion fleet before it landed rested with the RAF and the navy. The navy was one area where Britain had a substantial numerical superiority over the enemy, by a factor of about ten to one. But, in mid-1940, the Home Fleet was at its weakest for some time – only four of its eight capital ships were available at short notice and Dover and Portsmouth had only five destroyers each. The evidence of the early stages of the war also showed that it was seriously lacking in early warning of the enemy's intentions and vulnerable to air-and submarine-attack.

A fleet of about four hundred small boats was maintained around the coast from Invergordon to Portland, to provide not-particularly-early warning of an incoming invasion fleet. Throughout the summer of 1940, some two to three hundred vessels of various types were constantly on patrol in the main danger-area between The Wash and Sussex. Longer-range reconnaissance was provided by thirty-five submarines and aircraft, which operated a fixed pattern of patrols of varying intensity around the southern and eastern coastlines. The Admiralty was trying to cover a range of invasion options, from the east coast as far north as Scotland, to the possibility of a landing in Ireland.

One comfort was that the German navy was known to have been seriously weakened during the invasion of Norway. British intelligence at the time was not aware of the full extent of that weakness. Unbeknown to them, two of the Germans' key capital ships, the battle-cruisers *Scharnhorst* and *Gneisenau*, were both out of action owing to torpedo damage.

Britain, with its larger naval resources to draw upon, was also able to reinforce its Home Fleet more rapidly. By the end of July, Nore Command had increased its fleet of destroyers from nineteen to thirty-two (plus five corvettes). Many more vessels, including major capital ships, could potentially have been bought into action within hours in the event of a threatened invasion. Under normal circumstances, Admiral Pound considered it 'unsafe for a destroyer to be at sea by day anywhere between Portland and Dover' without air supremacy in the Channel. However, in the event of invasion, different rules would have applied. Even though the risks to the Royal Navy from the Luftwaffe and the coastal guns in the confined spaces of the Channel would have been huge, naval staff were confident that an attempted surprise crossing would be a 'most hazardous undertaking' for the Germans.

Coastal defences: the big guns

The Germans started installing a range of heavy guns along the opposite shore within a month of gaining control of it and there was soon a formidable range of guns trained on the Channel, and England beyond it. At the start of the war, Dover's heavy artillery consisted of just two 6-inch heavy guns, some 12-pounders and two 9.2-inch guns. All were of First World War vintage and the 12-pounders were of a design dating back to the 1880s. None of them had a cross-Channel capability.

Improvements in Dover's heavy weaponry started with the installation on St Margaret's Golf Course in August 1940 of the first of two 14-inch railway-mounted ex-naval guns, which were christened 'Winnie' (after the Prime Minister) and 'Pooh' (after the bear). However, these were hydraulically operated; they were too slow to track enemy shipping and, if used against land targets, they ran the risk of retaliation from the superior German guns. In addition, the huge forces generated by firing the guns meant that Winnie's barrel wore out after firing just fifty rounds. From November 1940, a 13.5-inch gun called 'Peacemaker' was deployed on an old colliery siding at Stone Hall, near Lydden. Its two companions were called 'Gladiator' and 'Sceneshifter'. The largest Allied gun, 'Bochebuster', fired 18-inch shells weighing 1 ton and standing 6 feet 7 inches high.

The best of the German guns was capable of shelling Maidstone, 55 miles from the French coast. This was done in 1944, it is thought in an attempt to disguise the arrival of the first V1 rockets. They and the Allies staged the first real cross-Channel artillery duel on 17 September 1944, as the Canadian forces went in to capture the gun emplacements on the Pas-de-Calais. Both Churchill and Hitler took a great deal of interest in their respective heavy batteries, but others (like Brooke) had considerable doubts about their military value:

> *These guns* (Winnie and Pooh) *were great pets of Winston, but to my mind the purpose they served did not warrant the personnel they absorbed.* Danchev and Todman, 4 March 1941

Dragon's teeth – concrete anti-tank obstacles – were produced and installed in vast numbers. From the position of these examples, it is not immediately obvious what their defensive purpose was.

An 18-inch railway-mounted gun demonstrates its potential – as seating.

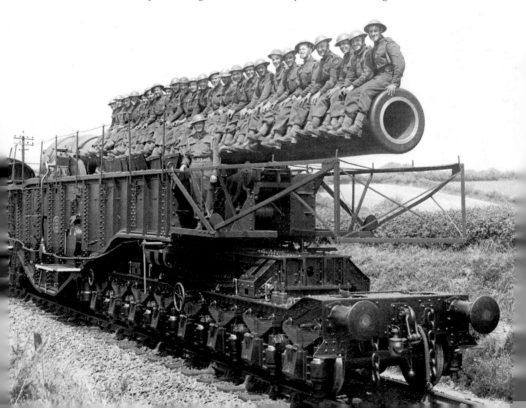

A 9.2-inch mobile gun awaits the call to action from its siding on the Southern Railway.

Port and other coastal defences

As long ago as the early 1920s, the Admiralty had drawn up a list of some thirty ports needing protection against all possible forms of attack, from long-range bombardment to landings of invading forces. The defences were to be provided by mine barrages, anti-submarine booms and naval guns, and the main ports within our area to be so protected included Dover, Newhaven and the Thames/Medway area. Following Dunkirk, in addition to the major ports, there was also protection for some thirteen minor ports and forty-five beaches along the south coast that offered a promising landing ground. This often took the form of mothballed guns from derelict warships scrapped since the First World War.

A first batch of forty-six batteries was installed at key points along the coast in June 1940. Some had to be manned initially by sailors, because of the shortage of suitably trained army personnel. Attempts were made to camouflage the guns and, in order to save ammunition and to preserve the element of surprise until the last possible moment, the gunners were told not to open fire until the enemy were within 3 to 4 miles – about half their effective range.

Few concessions were made to the comfort of those who had to man these batteries:

> *The site where half of us... ended up was immeasurably the worst of the lot – adrift in a sea of mud reminiscent of Passchendaele, without a functioning cookhouse or any washing or cooking facilities whatsoever. The hut into which some forty of us were dumped in mid-November was innocent of window glass, lighting, heating or paint. It was also completely bedless, so we made do with straw-filled palliasses and about three feet of space per man.* Quoted in Humphreys, *Hellfire Corner*, p. 35

The men on this particular battery subsisted in this manner throughout the winter, with toilet facilities consisting of galvanised buckets behind sacking screens, and food cooked on coal fires, which was served lukewarm and tasting strongly of soot. They were also given alarming instructions for defending their part of the coastline (this was in May, 1940):

> *To cap it all, we were given the interesting news that there were no other troops between Pegwell Bay and Dover. In the event of an invasion the defence of that line was down to us. With just six rifles and a dozen or so pickaxe helves, the chances of a spirited resistance seemed rather on the thin side. Incidentally, none of us had ever fired a rifle, and we had only fifty rounds between us anyway. Our officers instructed us that should paratroops land, we were to rush at them with the pickaxe helves, stun them and grab their guns.* Peter Erwood, quoted in Humphreys, *Hellfire Corner*, pp. 36-7

Some of the coastal anti-invasion weapons used by the regular army were almost as improvised as their Home Guard counterparts. A supply of 40lb RAF bombs was kept on top of the cliffs at Dover Castle. In the event of a German landing, they were simply to be hurled over the cliff edge onto the beach below.

But the most frightening decision about coastal defences was made in secret. In the event of a German landing proving to be successful, aircraft were to be used to bomb the beaches with mustard gas. Production of the gas was stepped up and exercises in dropping it were actually carried out, using a pink powder in place of the gas itself. This was a particularly high-risk strategy, given the likelihood that the Germans would retaliate in kind. A group of soldiers in Dover learned something of the potency of this weapon. After working with the gas, they visited the lavatory without first washing their hands properly. They suffered burns that

Soldiers take a well-earned dip at 'a seaside resort'. The improvised coastal defences can be seen in the background.

were painful and embarrassing in equal measure, and needed hospital treatment of a confidential nature.

Minefields formed part of the defence of the coastline, and they could prove to be as hazardous to the British as to the enemy. One soldier boasted that he knew the way through the minefield on the ridge at Farthingloe, and proved himself fatally wrong. In another incident, an army car had brake failure and finally came to a halt in the middle of a minefield. Its occupants passed a nervous night in the car before engineers came to rescue them. The Canadians also laid a minefield on the Western Heights at Dover but neglected to make a note of where exactly it was.

Where minefields were known about, the normal practice was to erect a barbed-wire barrier immediately behind them: first, to make it more difficult for invaders to get off the beach and, second, to stop innocent people and animals wandering into it. The first was happily never tested but the second was not always successful, and a number of fatalities were recorded.

Anti-tank defences were improvised on the beaches, using scaffolding poles. The 7th Battalion of the Wiltshire Regiment were responsible for building the section between Milford-on-Sea and Highcliffe, and even the process of erecting it was frightening enough:

> *The scaffoldings were quite large structures, clamped together on the beach and carried bodily out into the sea by twenty-five of us, when the tide was at its lowest* (often 3 or 5 am in November). *We used to go blue with the cold on moonlit nights and had Thermos urns of cocoa provided for us. When a long line of obstacles were carried out to sea, all the tall men had to carry the shorter men out to join the sections together with further clamps and steel scaffolding. Sometimes the waves went right over our heads and it was indeed a very frightening experience to those of us who could not swim (sadly I couldn't). So we had to let go and jump up to gasp for a breath of air.* Henry Wills. *Pillboxes: A Study of UK Defences 1940,* Leo Cooper, 1985, pp. 54-5

Napoleonic defences

The defence of Dover and the strait it overlooked took on special importance. From August 1939, it was under the control of Vice-Admiral Bertram Ramsay, who had been brought out of retirement to take up the post. He occupied as his headquarters the easternmost casemate tunnel, dug into the cliffs below Dover Castle by French prisoners in 1797. From here, he co-ordinated the rescue of the Allied troops from Dunkirk in 1940. The tunnels were extended in 1941, partly to provide accommodation for the Post Office and their telecommunications. By 1943, the tunnels became a combined headquarters for all three services and played an important part in the planning of D-Day, serving as a duplicate headquarters in the event that the main operations centre at Portsmouth was knocked out.

Within the castle was kept a book detailing the plans for the defence of the town in the event of an invasion – which bridges were to be demolished, where points were protected by fougasses, and so on. In essence, the desperate message was that the bridges would be blown and that every man would then be expected to fight to his last round.

Vice-Admiral Sir Bertram Ramsay, Commander of the defences at Dover and the mastermind behind Operation Dynamo, *the evacuation from Dunkirk. He is commemorated in Dover Castle, scene of his triumphs.*

The Royal Military Canal was another Napoleonic remain that would have provided a significant barrier to forces in 1940.

Two other features of Napoleonic vintage were pressed into use as part of the coastal defences. Seventy-four Martello towers were built on the south coast between Folkestone and Seaford, west of Eastbourne, in 1805. They would originally have had a large cannon on top. They formed part of the Second World War defences for this part of the coast, with their artillery suitably updated. Despite their age, they would have been a formidable defensive position; their walls on the seaward side were up to 13 feet thick. Built at about the same time, the Royal Military Canal ran for 28 miles, between Hythe and Rye. It too was an impressive piece of military engineering, some 60 feet wide with a 13-foot-high earth parapet behind it, and so designed as to allow the artillery behind to defend it with maximum effect.

The Martello towers, built along the coast to guard against Napoleon, were updated to keep out Hitler's forces a century and a half later.

The army

Brooke's revised home-defence plans, prepared in July, had largely been implemented by September. Most of the mobile reserves were kept behind a line from The Wash to Newhaven. In front of that, much would depend upon the navy and air force stopping the invaders before they got ashore and local garrisons dealing with the remainder – the prospect of support in numbers from the general reserve was still far from immediate. These reserves consisted of two corps. The nearest to Kent and Sussex was the VII Corps, based in Surrey and comprising the 1st Canadian Division, the 1st Armoured Division and 1 Army Tank Brigade.

In the south-east, the plans involved the identification of what were variously called 'fortress towns', 'anti-tank islands' or 'nodal points'. Rootes explains the strategy:

> *An outer perimeter at each of the towns would be manned by regular troops and members of the Home Guard in the event of an enemy attack; civilian evacuation would end immediately once such an attack began; and when the fighting became fiercer, the soldiers were to fall back to an inner perimeter, sometimes known as a 'keep'. Such a town was expected to hold out for a week, giving reinforcements time to reach the scene, it was hoped, or at least delaying the enemy's advance.*
> Andrew Rootes. *Front Line County,* Robert Hale, 1980, p. 192

The following towns in Kent had been given this defensive role by November 1941: Canterbury, Chatham, Deal, Dover, Faversham, Folkestone, Maidstone, Margate, Ramsgate, Sittingbourne and Tunbridge Wells. Most of the county's other main towns were allocated a lower (Category B) status, but were still expected to hold out for at least two days. Rootes details the defensive measures put in place around Ashford: deepening the River Stour; 3 miles of anti-tank obstacles; 1 mile of dynamited pipeline that could be detonated to provide an instant anti-tank ditch; fifty roadblocks; five rail blocks; thirty-two machine-gun and anti-tank positions. They would be manned by 1,300 regular troops and 700 Home Guards. The inner perimeter would have been the last redoubt, where the defending forces would have been expected to fight, if necessary, to the last man. In Maidstone, the area around the Town Hall – High Street, Mill Street and Palace Avenue – would have been the scene of that final desperate battle.

In each town, a triumvirate of military commander, police officer and local authority representative was established to ensure co-ordination of the civil and military authorities. Emergency food and water supplies were laid on and efforts would be made to evacuate non-essential civilians. Across the coastal belt of Kent as a whole, this would have meant moving out all but 6,500 of the 215,000 population. Above all, it would be an organised evacuation, and plans were also in place to prevent panic migrations – by force, if necessary.

Pillboxes

Today, pillboxes are perhaps the most visible reminder of Britain's defensive plans in 1940. The army was desperately short of tanks, especially after Dunkirk and the subsequent evacuations, and had no prospect of making up the shortfall quickly. But a pillbox with a large-calibre weapon in it is, in effect, a tank without the tracks.

This map, taken from the book Pillboxes: A Study of UK Defences 1940 by Henry Wills, shows the main defensive lines in Kent and Sussex and the pillboxes along them.

(Reversing the roles, both sides at different stages in the war used the tactic of digging a tank into a fortified position – making it, in effect, a pillbox **with** tracks.)

Experience of them in the early stages of the war was not encouraging. When the British Expeditionary Force landed in France to defend the Valenciennes to Armentières sector of the Belgian border, they found it almost totally unfortified. They set out to replicate something as near as possible to the Maginot Line in the time available, and over 400 pillboxes and 40 miles of anti-tank ditch were constructed in the seven months between their arrival and the rude interruption of their works by the Germans. Similar stop lines formed a central part of Ironside's home-defence strategy, with lines of pillboxes at key points on the enemy's route inland (see map). But when they were tested against the invading panzers, they were found to do no more than delay them.

Nonetheless, construction of pillboxes at home proceeded at a furious pace in 1940. By late July, 8,000 had been completed and a further 17,000 were under construction. Army Commands sent out surveying teams to identify suitable defensive lines and work out appropriate measures along them. They also decided which bridges and other structures to wire with explosives, further to impede the

This pillbox at Kingsworth was sufficiently well disguised as a garage to fool aerial reconnaissance, but was unlikely to pass closer inspection.

enemy's progress. The 1939 Defence Regulations permitted the authorities to use private land, but also ruled that compensation was payable to the owner, based on the loss in value of their land.

Orders would then be issued to contractors to build the pillboxes to the standard War Office specifications. Unfortunately, the timescale for building these structures, and the location and circumstances of their construction, could be anything but normal. One contractor was asked to build 200 pillboxes along 50 miles of coast within three weeks!

One of the consequences of this vast amount of building was a national shortage of building materials. Later investigations showed that the steel reinforcement of pillboxes sometimes took the form of park railings or even bedsprings. Cement was also in short supply and compromises were made, in terms of thinner walls where direct hits were not expected and the omission of concrete floors to the pillboxes. Some defence schemes even had to be abandoned, owing to the lack of cement.

But it was in the camouflage of pillboxes that the nation's genius for improvisation found its fullest expression. The British pillbox was to be found in almost every guise, adding surprise to their normal military capabilities. They included: house extensions; Victorian 'follies'; roadside garages (complete with dummy petrol pump); part of a coal-yard; pseudo-ancient additions to Pevensey Castle; a bus shelter (complete with timetable); kiosks and bookstalls. W H Smith had a branch they may not have known about on the beach at Margate and another stall had the giveaway proprietor's name 'Hyam Ready'. In similar vein, one at Woodbridge was concealed behind a hoarding advertising the 'Hotel Continental: Warm welcome for visiting troops.' Another team went to great pains to disguise one with signs advertising a public convenience, then realised that, if the invaders could not read English, all their work would have been in vain. There were haystacks, summerhouses, railway wagons, motor vans, bathing cubicles, roundabouts, chalets and clumps of bushes. Elstree Film Studios were called in to produce canvas mock-ups of stone walls. Pillboxes were hung from the underside of seaside piers and railway bridges.

Even during the construction period, the workers had to be aware of the dangers of German photographic reconnaissance. Tracks to the site had to be hidden from view; light-coloured spoil-heaps painted; areas of barbed-wire around pillboxes, where the grass might grow long and uncut, had to be disguised. There were also some 200 dummy pillboxes constructed in the Eastern Command area alone for the Germans to spot, until it was realised that they were costing almost as much as the real thing.

Even ancient Pevensey Castle had disguised pillboxes inserted into its walls.

Anti-aircraft defences

> *The nation's anti-aircraft defences were not in good shape at the outbreak of war. During the inter-war years they had been very much the Cinderella of the armed forces, not least on the grounds that they had very little hope of actually hitting anything.* Stuart Hylton. *Their Darkest Hour,* Sutton, 2001, p. 85

According to the wartime Anti-Aircraft Command, a field gun aiming at a static target had a one-in-a-hundred chance of scoring a direct hit. Even these long odds were hugely increased when aiming at a high-flying aircraft; in the twenty to thirty seconds it took the shell to travel from gun to target, a plane might travel a further 2 miles. Small wonder that, in a 1926 exercise, firing at a plane obligingly flying at a steady course and a known speed, the gunners scored just 2 hits out of 2,935 shots. Their cause was not helped by the fact that aircraft technology (in terms of their height and speed), whilst having remained relatively static in the years 1918 to 1932, then made major leaps forward. The guns, already at a considerable disadvantage, then had a lot more catching up to do. In September 1940, the anti-aircraft guns brought down just one German plane for every 30,000 shells they fired.

The First World War vintage 3-inch guns, on which British anti-aircraft defences relied heavily in 1939, did not have sufficient range to trouble the new German

The Bofors gun was introduced early in the war to deal with lower-flying enemy aircraft.

bombers at their maximum operational heights. The best they could hope to do was to force the bombers higher, which had the effect of slowing them down. Small surprise, then, that the inter-war anti-aircraft regiments were hugely undermanned (in one case, 30 men to cover 150 posts) and under-resourced (some ended up buying their own equipment, rather than wait forever for it to be provided). The rise of Hitler had prompted a belated reappraisal; by 1936, Britain's first anti-aircraft division had been formed and, by 1938, five divisions had been bought together into a corps, under General Sir Frederick Pile.

Newer 3.7-inch and 4.5-inch guns were starting to be introduced by 1939. They had the theoretical range to reach the attackers, but their effective ceiling (the maximum height at which they could engage the attacker for a reasonable period of time – say twenty to thirty seconds) was something like 3,000-5,000 feet less than their theoretical maximum range. However, they did represent a quantum leap in fire-power, as is illustrated by the first experience of a crew at Dover firing theirs, early in the war:

> *There was a moment's silence, then a huge flash and stupendous bang as the four guns fired in perfect salvo... I had braced myself for some noise but this was something else. The earth shook and various constructional defects in our dugout became immediately apparent. A large part of the roof fell on top of my unfortunate co-telephonist.* Peter Erwood, quoted in Humphreys, *Hellfire Corner*, p. 39

Anti-aircraft technology made great strides during the war years, and by 1943 the gunners had electronic means of early warning, the ability to identify friend or foe and to predict the future position of an aircraft and the necessary trajectory of a shell to meet it. The following year saw the introduction of the proximity fuse, a miniature radar-operated device, which detected the presence of a plane nearby and detonated the shell. This improved the 'kill' rate to one plane for each 4,000 shells. For lower-flying aircraft, a smaller, faster-firing gun was needed. The 40mm Bofors gun was introduced in 1940 as the standard light anti-aircraft gun, with a range of up to 5,000 feet. It was used to defend ports, airfields and other key installations.

One great strength of the anti-aircraft defences was their mobility. Within two days of the attacks on London starting in September 1940, General Pile was able to bring in every spare gun in the country for the defence of the city, doubling his fire-power and encasing London in 'a curtain of steel and iron'. After D-Day, anti-aircraft defences were again moved virtually overnight (in Operation *Diver*), to create the Kentish Gun Belt, a line of 376 heavy anti-aircraft guns and 576 Bofors guns in a line reaching from Faversham to Crawley, as a defence against the new threat of the V1 flying bombs. When this did not work, (partly due to conflicts between the guns and RAF pilots pursuing the bombs) they were moved again, to form a coastal gun belt stretching from Dover to Seaford. It says much for the improved accuracy of anti-aircraft gunnery that, in their most successful week, the service claimed an 82 per cent success rate against the V1s.

For all that they were there to defend the civilian population, anti-aircraft crews were not always welcome when they set up in residential areas. Some feared that the location of a searchlight or a gun would bring down the wrath of the Luftwaffe on their street. The residents' fears were not entirely unfounded. The intensity of anti-aircraft fire put up around Manston and Hawkinge airfields during the raids on 15 August 1940 led to the towns of Ramsgate and Broadstairs getting bombs that were intended for the RAF. Shrapnel from the shells or, worse, faulty shells exploding when they landed, added to the dangers for the locality. In London, there were as many civilians killed by anti-aircraft ordnance as by enemy bombing.

The searchlights that came with the guns were used for much more than just spotting enemy bombers; they would guide RAF personnel home; spot ditched crew members in the sea; mark the location of mines dropped in coastal waters and light up barrage balloons to stop Allied planes colliding with them. They were, however, subject to significant limitations. They often did not have enough range to find the planes, generally not working much above 12,000 feet, and in any event found it hard to track planes that were within their reach, relying as they did in the early stages of the war upon acoustic methods of tracking, with their built-in time-lag. Similar limitations existed for the coastal guns, some of which at night could only be used at a third of their full operational range, due to the inadequacies of their lights. Some of those lining the Thames Estuary had no lights at all, and were consequently useless after dark.

Home Guards eventually took over much of the manning of these batteries and, in time, they were joined by the women of the ATS. This led to an unusual row over rations; the ATS were doing the same physical work as the men, but were being given smaller rations. The dispute was eventually resolved by pooling the rations

A rather war-worn barrage balloon is launched near to what appears to be an equally war-worn oast-house.

and sharing them out equally to all personnel. As the contemporary official record quaintly puts it:

> *Special regard was paid to the women's need for fresh fruit, salads and milk foods; and a balance was found between this and the spotted dog and cheese and pickles beloved of the old soldier – or the new soldier, for that matter.* Roof over Britain: the Official Story of Britain's Anti-aircraft Defences 1939-42, HMSO, 1943, p. 59

One unexpected impact of the advent of women AA gun-crews was on the 'sex' of barrage balloons. These had hitherto tended to be named (rather unflatteringly) after women, but the advent of women crews led to 'male' balloons.

The Germans tried fitting a form of balloon deflector on their bombers, but these fenders weighed 800lb and seriously affected the performance of their planes. Balloons were also used on board ships to protect convoys passing through the Dover Strait. During the later stages of the war, a dense barrage of balloons was put up between Gravesend and Sevenoaks, to help catch any V1s that escaped the attention of the guns and fighters. This was subsequently extended, to cover the area between Cobham in Kent and Limpsfield (Surrey). However, our balloons were no less of a hazard to Allied aircraft and, according to Hayward, four times as many RAF planes as Luftwaffe fell victim to them.

Airfield defences

The defence of airfields became a bone of contention between the services. The army shared responsibility for their defence with the air force, who argued for them to be given greater priority. The air force feared that the Germans might use paratroops to immobilise key airfields – at least temporarily – during an invasion, denying the other services vital air cover. They wanted some of the best soldiers, with the most up-to-date weapons, guarding those airfields. These were the same troops who were in such short supply as mobile counter-offensive forces. Ironside, visiting the airfield at Northolt, noted in his diary that it had good defences, but deplored the fact that there were 2,000 unarmed air personnel on the site, who should have been training to help in its defence.

An uneasy compromise was eventually found to this last problem, by issuing RAF personnel with rifles and reinforcing them with local troops (and thus possibly adding the confusion of different chains of command to their problems). Perhaps the most hand-to-mouth example of this approach was to be seen in the desperate days of early September 1940, on Hawkinge airfield (which was actually visible from German-occupied France). Every person on the airfield – down to cooks and filing clerks – was issued with a rifle and five rounds of ammunition and was told, in the event of invasion to make every shot count, since there was no more ammunition available.

Pillboxes on airfields could present new problems – not least that the aircraft might crash into them. Various ingenious methods were devised to get round this. The Pickett-Hamilton Counterbalance Fort spent most of its time flush with the ground – looking like a circle of concrete with a manhole cover set into it. When required, its five-man crew would climb in and, within four seconds, raise it to its

THE TETT TURRET

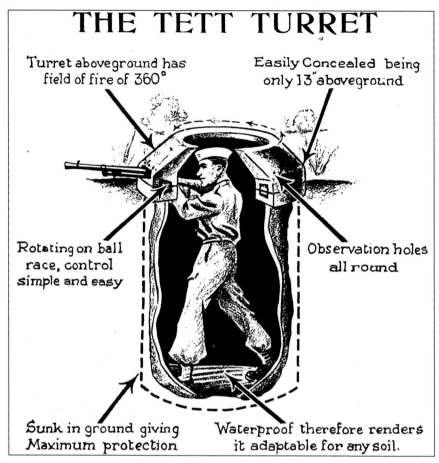

Turret aboveground has field of fire of 360°

Easily Concealed being only 13" aboveground

Rotating on ball race, control simple and easy

Observation holes all round

Sunk in ground giving Maximum protection

Waterproof therefore renders it adaptable for any soil.

The Tett Turret – the adverts spoke highly of it, but it was not popular with those who had to use it.

operational height with the aid of a standard garage jack (later versions had a compressed-air lifting device). In a further ten seconds it could be lowered again and the airfield returned to full operational use. Winston Churchill saw a demonstration of these and was thereafter their enthusiastic champion. A number of airfields were fitted with them, but they were prone to flooding and unpopular with the troops.

Another approach to the problem was the low-level cantilevered concrete pillbox. This was flush enough to the ground not to interfere with most aircraft, unless they landed directly on top of it, and also gave a 360-degree field of fire. A further variation was the Tett Turret, essentially a length of 4-foot-diameter concrete drainpipe sunk into the ground. Only the top 13 inches showed above the ground, where the two occupants operated a revolving top. This model was not popular. It too was prone to flooding and its confined accommodation resulted in the occupants going down with cramp if they stayed in there for long. It was also dangerous getting in and out of it if the enemy were in the vicinity. Small wonder that a slit trench was felt to offer similar amenities at a much lower cost.

The other option was the mobile pillbox. Various manufacturers produced pillboxes that could be mounted on the back of a civilian lorry. The so-called Bison tank could hold between ten and twenty men, in what looked like a garden shed but which offered the protection of 4 inches of reinforced concrete. (However, the lorry itself does not appear to have been in any way armoured. In the event of an attack, the pillbox could not have been expected to remain mobile for long).

One of the more bizarre forms of airfield defence was the unrotated missile, or PAC, which stood for 'Parachute and Cable'. This consisted of a series of large firework-type rockets, fired from tubes, to which were attached about 1,000 feet of cable. At the top of its trajectory, a parachute would be released from the rocket and at the other end was another parachute and a small mine. The idea was that the airfield would be ringed with these and, at the appropriate moment, they would be fired into the air and would wrap themselves around the attackers' wings, the mine bringing the plane down. A number of airfields, including Manston and Biggin Hill, had these installed, but there is only one authenticated report of them bringing down a German plane.

Equally ingenious, and rather more effective, were the dummy airfields set up near the real ones and designed to lure attackers away. Some (the K sites) were designed to look like the nearby original by day, with the field patterns of the mother airfield replicated (painted on the ground) and dummy aircraft and buildings; others (the Q sites) were simply patterns of lights, designed to simulate runway lighting at night. To fool later reconnaissance flights, artificial 'bomb craters' were painted on canvas and laid out on the undamaged runways of the real airfield, while the actual craters on the decoy were quickly patched up. There were different bomb-crater canvases; ones with shadows for sunny days and those without for dull ones – and the shadows would even be rotated to keep them in line with the movement of the sun. By August 1940, there were twenty-six K and fifty-six Q sites in existence, and between them they attracted sixty attacks from the Luftwaffe. Other night-time decoys, known as QF sites, were designed to lure bombers away from urban targets. They had a range of small lights showing, such as one might expect to see over an urban area, and had the facility to start larger fires going, to simulate bomb damage. Ingenious though they were, the cost of the K sites told against them, and they did not have as great a diverting effect as the cheaper Q sites. Most were abandoned by 1942, though further elaborate decoys were used in the run-up to D-Day, to persuade the Germans that the invasion would come, first in 1943, and then in 1944 in the area of Calais.

Some airfield defences were improvised in the extreme. Manston had a home-made armoured car fitted with a Lewis gun, along with Browning machine guns from their Blenheim night-fighters on various ingenious mountings, while Tangmere used captured German machine guns from a Stuka. The defenders of Manston were at one point even reduced to firing Very pistols at the attacking planes.

Radar

In the 1930s, military planners despaired of finding countermeasures to the bomber. The big problem for fighter planes, the obvious deterrent, was that of getting sufficient notice of the bombers to get airborne in time, climb to altitude and then find them. The visual methods used in the First World War were made redundant by the increased speed of aircraft. Between the wars, experiments were carried out with acoustic listening devices – concrete dishes up to 30 feet in diameter and even – at Greatstone, near Dungeness – an 80-yard curved wall, all of them designed to reflect aircraft noise onto a microphone. However, these could be drowned out by ships' engines, wind, wave noise or any other disturbance. One demonstration in front of Air Chief Marshal Dowding was ruined when a milkman's cart rattled along the horizon. Even under ideal conditions, they did not have sufficient range to get the fighters aloft and into combat positions in time.

In desperation, military planners turned to the fanciful notion of some kind of death ray, something that would incapacitate either the aircrew or the plane itself. One of the men they approached was the 42-year-old head of the Wireless Research Station at the National Physical Laboratory.

Up to that time, Robert Watson-Watt's work had concentrated on identifying atmospheric disturbances as an aid to weather forecasting. He was unable to help them with death rays, but he had noticed the propensity of aircraft to interrupt his experiments by reflecting back radio signals. It was a widely known phenomenon, but Watson-Watt recognised its potential for detecting aircraft. He put the idea to the Ministry in February 1935 and a test proved successful beyond all expectations. However, not all demonstrations went as smoothly. One in 1936 was a complete failure, due to the use of an incorrect frequency, and their distinguished guests (Sir Henry Tizard and Air Chief Marshal Dowding) stormed out, Dowding calling the project's chief engineer 'a charlatan'! The funding for radar was nearly lost that day

The acoustic wall at Greatstone, near Dungeness, built to reflect the sound of incoming aircraft onto microphones. Work on it was abandoned as radar was introduced.

The radar masts at Swingate, near Dover, still survive to this day. They were not easily hidden from the Germans.

and, with it, possibly, the war. But after that, things happened quickly. By June, a trial station had been built at Aldeburgh, Suffolk, and the Government, in an unusual show of decisiveness, allocated the massive sum of £10 millions for Watson-Watt's grand scheme – the Chain Home stations. By the outbreak of war a series of seventeen stations, each with a range of 100 miles, ringed the coast. Those within Kent and Sussex were at Pevensey, Rye, Dover and Dunkirk, near Canterbury.

One problem with these was that, due to the curvature of the earth, these stations could not detect low-flying aircraft. Low-altitude attacks could still achieve almost complete surprise, as the pilots at RAF Hawkinge were to find out in August 1940, when Stukas started bombing the airfield before they had even been scrambled. A further twenty-four stations – the Chain Home Low stations – were developed to fill this gap (including stations at Poling, Truleigh, Beachy Head, Fairlight, Dover and Foreness). They used a different wavelength (1.5 metres) and different masts, and their maximum range of detection was shorter. From late 1941 onwards, there were also Chain Home Extra Low stations, which had the option of being mobile, mounted on a standard lorry chassis.

They were referred to in public as Radio Direction Finding stations, a familiar technology whose defence implications were not immediately evident from the name. However, 100-metre-high masts spread along the coast were likely to be noticed by enemy intelligence so, before the war, the authorities also spread the word that they were connected with the new television service that the BBC had launched in November 1936. Military personnel at the stations wore the insignia AMES – Air Ministry Experimental Section – and rumours grew up in the neighbouring communities that the stations had the power to direct rockets at incoming planes, or send secret rays that could stop a bomber's engines. On 2 August 1939, the *Graf Zeppelin* had made a silent and stately progress up the length of the eastern coast of England. It is now known that it was loaded with scientific equipment designed to detect the presence of radar. For a series of technical reasons, it failed to detect the British stations and this was to have major significance for the outcome of the war.

As important as radar itself was the fact that the British developed the communications infrastructure to put the new technology to full use. Dedicated land-lines linked the stations to communications centres, from where fighter squadrons could be scrambled and directed to their targets by radio telephone. Not even all of the British pilots were in on the secret of radar, and some of them marvelled at the uncanny ability of their controllers to lead them to the enemy. The destruction of that communications infrastructure could have had as much, or even more impact on the effectiveness of Britain's defences than the damage to the radar stations themselves. Air Chief Marshal Sir Keith Park, the head of 11 Group during the Battle of Britain, put it in these terms:

> *There were more airfields in the south not belonging to Fighter Command yet available to us, but they did not have good signals, and without signals the only thing I commanded was my desk at Uxbridge.* Group Captain J E Johnson. *Full Circle: the Tactics of Air Fighting 1914-1964*, Ballantine, 1964, p. 174

Important as it was, the margin of warning that radar gave to our fighters was a very fine one. The Kent radar could give at best twenty minutes' notice of an attack. Four of those minutes were spent getting the warning from the radar station to the operations table of Fighter Command. Squadrons could then be scrambled, but it took a Spitfire thirteen and a Hurricane sixteen minutes to climb to a height of 20,000 feet. One of the consequences of this was that it was not possible to assemble 'big wings' of three or four squadrons (36-48 planes) to take on the German *Gruppe* (their operational unit of 30 planes), often leaving the British pilots outnumbered.

Despite Goering's scepticism that the British had any effective form of early warning, the Luftwaffe on 12 August launched a series of attacks against the stations at Dover, Dunkirk (near Canterbury), Pevensey, Rye and Ventnor. Of these, only Ventnor suffered long-term damage. For a number of reasons, radar stations were difficult to bomb; the open-lattice structure of the masts made them resistant to anything but a direct hit, and accurate dive-bombing was difficult, since their height and design made them an awkward target. The stations themselves (at least, those on the east coast) were designed with protected buildings, surrounded by earth banks and with concrete roofs protected with a 1.7-metre-thick layer of shingle, to dissipate any bomb blast. These latter were not totally bomb-proof. One building at the Dover station suffered a direct hit on its concrete roof, which cracked and filled the commanding officer's room to the ceiling with shingle (he was fortunately out at the time). There were also duplicate buildings, either underground or in remote locations, and a back-up generator in case mains power were lost. Even so, had the Germans persevered, there is no doubt that they would have eventually put the stations out of service, and the eyes of the RAF would have been lost. But Goering cancelled any further raids on them within days of the first one, declaring them a waste of bombs and bombers. He may have been fooled into doing so in part by the fact that the British brought in equipment to continue transmitting dummy signals from Ventnor after its bombing, leading the Germans to think that their raid had failed and that it was still operational.

Once the enemy had crossed the coast and was heading inland, they went out of radar signal (the radar aerials pointed out to sea). It then fell to the Royal Observer Corps to track the course and height of the attackers. Churchill rather unkindly likened this handover to 'a transition from the middle of the twentieth

This is thought to be the aftermath of a Luftwaffe raid on the radar station at Swingate, near Dover.

century to the early Stone Age', since it meant a return to identifying planes by audible and visual signals. The corps manned some 1,400 posts nationally (about 50 of them in Kent), generally on a part-time, volunteer basis. They would call in reports of sightings of both Allied and enemy planes to the operations room, which would in turn alert gun and light teams. They relied on the old technology of acoustic detection, discussed earlier. Later in the war, additional radar stations were built to cover this gap.

It is difficult to overstate the importance of radar to the Allied cause during the Battle of Britain. Using it, the Allied fighters, with the aid of their controllers, could 'see' 120 miles. This enabled them (as far as the technology linking the radar site and the fighter permitted) to be in the right position to meet the incoming enemy. Their German counterparts were limited to the 4 or 5 miles visible from their cockpits.

Intelligence

> *The intelligence available on the military preparedness of the island and on the coastal defences is meagre and not very reliable. Field Marshal Keitel, 7 July 1940. The difficulty of obtaining information is increased by the fact that there is little actual contact with the enemy land forces.* General Staff MI14. 'Notes on German Preparations for Invasion of the United Kingdom'

One big difference the Channel did make was in the amount of intelligence available to either of the forces at the front line. Sneaking over to take a look meant a major and hazardous expedition, and those enemy troops who did fall into the hands of the other side often had the great disadvantage that they had been drowned.

On 31 May a sub-committee of the Joint Intelligence Committee, the Invasion Warning Sub-Committee, met for the first time. Given that their task was to gather evidence of imminent invasion, that was what they did, regardless of whether or not the evidence was there to be gathered. At its first meeting it was told that 'extensive German plans for a descent on Eire have been in preparation for a considerable time,' and they received a report from the officer commanding the naval shore establishment at Dover, Vice-Admiral Ramsay, saying:

> *Indications of numerous acts of sabotage and Fifth Column activity* [are evident] *in Dover, e.g. communications leakages, fixed defences sabotage, second-hand cars purchased at fantastic prices and left at various parking places.* Fleming, p. 62

The British authorities wasted no opportunity to fan the flames of hysteria which grew up around the shadowy menace of the fifth column. General Ironside, speaking to a meeting of senior LDV commanders on 5 June, said:

> *We have got examples of where there have been people quite definitely preparing aerodromes in this country... We want to know from you what is going on. Is there anything peculiar happening? Are there any peculiar people?* Fleming, p. 62

In the fevered atmosphere of 1940, there was no shortage of 'peculiar people' waiting to be unmasked by vigilant citizens, but even the almost total absence of hard evidence did not shake the authorities' conviction that fifth column activity was going on. Ironside again:

> *It is extraordinary how we get circumstantial reports of Fifth Columnists and yet we have never been able to get anything worth having. One is persuaded that it hardly exists. And yet there is signalling going on all over the place and we cannot get any evidence.* Hylton, p.4

The authorities published guidance on who the public should take orders from, and how a real official might be distinguished from an imposter. Tests were introduced, getting suspects to say words that were difficult for Germans to pronounce (which tended to be bad news for Polish allies in the forces).

The Germans were naturally delighted at this recruiting campaign being run on their behalf by the British authorities, and took every opportunity to whip up the hysteria that it was creating. Their clandestine New British Broadcasting Station (purporting to be the voice of patriotic but disenchanted Britons) claimed on 9 August that they were going to send a force of 10,000 planes to drop 100,000 paratroops dressed in British uniforms captured in France, and others dressed (rather incongruously) as miners.

The British authorities had a fairly dismal record in intelligence-gathering. In the run-up to the war, they failed to forecast the reoccupation of the Rhineland or the invasion of Austria, though they did predict twenty other major moves by the Axis powers (eighteen of which did not happen). In consequence, on the rare occasions they did get something right, their political and military masters tended not to believe them. Naval Staff produced a detailed paper showing how the invasion would focus on the east coast. This strongly influenced British thinking for months afterwards, even as the fleets of invasion barges were seen to be building up in the Channel ports. As early as 21 June, the Invasion Warning Sub-Committee received accurate accounts of the plans for Operation *Sea Lion*, first from the German Military Attaché in Ankara via a Turkish staff officer, and then direct from the British Ambassador in Bucharest. They chose to ignore them.

Happily, the Germans were equally ignorant of what was going in England. In Germany, two agencies competed for the role of intelligence-gathering – the *Abwehr*, the intelligence wing of the armed forces, and the *Sicherheitsdienst*, part of the Nazi Party apparatus. Neither had made adequate preparations for establishing a network of agents in Britain before the war, on the grounds that Hitler had promised them that no war would take place before 1944/45. Such ill-prepared agents as they had in place were swiftly rounded up in the first days of the war, or by the subsequent general internment of enemy aliens. There are also accounts of their comically inept attempts to put agents ashore.

A classic of its kind was the party landed near Rye and Dungeness on 2 and 3 September 1940. It comprised two Dutchmen (one half-Japanese, which also made him rather prominent in this part of Kent), a German and another of uncertain origins. Only one had a fluent command of English and all were drunk. They carried incriminating equipment, including radios, which was clearly of German origin and were ill-briefed about English ways. Their English-speaker, for example, was detained when he tried to buy cider from a public house at breakfast time in defiance of the licensing laws. Another agent arrived in the village of Camber-on-Sea, near Hastings. All place-names had been obliterated but the sign above the Post Office read:

TUNBRIDGE
POST OFFICE AND STORES

This was a result of the fact that a Mr Tunbridge was the proprietor of the establishment, but this did not stop the *Abwehr* questioning the accuracy of the Ordnance Survey, which showed both Tonbridge and Tunbridge Wells lying some 30 miles inland. It will come as no surprise that such agents were generally rounded up quickly, and those who were not executed were sometimes 'turned' and operated as double agents.

For their part, the OKH (*Oberkommando des Heeres* – the Army Command) produced a map showing their intelligence of the strength and locations of the British forces in late September, when the invasion was originally due to take place. They managed to identify only five of thirty-seven divisions in their correct locations, put nine in completely the wrong area (one of the divisions they would have faced in Kent, they had down as being in Wales), could not find another five at all and identified the locations of eight completely non-existent divisions.

War by petrol

More imaginative, if not always very practicable, ideas for defences were also hatched in these challenging times. A whole Department of Petroleum Warfare was created under Geoffrey Lloyd, the Minister for Petroleum, in July 1940. This was dedicated to 'burning the invader back into the sea.' They dreamed up: the Static Flame Trap, a device for flooding suitable stretches of road with petrol and setting it ablaze with a Molotov cocktail (the most successful example of which was said to be at Dumpton Gap in Kent); the Flame Fougasse, which fired a mass of burning and sticky liquid from a 40-gallon drum hidden in the hedgerow onto any passing tank; the Hedgehopper, for lobbing burning projectiles down on passing invaders, where the topography on either side of the road permitted it (they had an alarming tendency to bounce back); and tank traps – ditches filled with inflammable liquids or petrol-soaked peat. Some of their devices, such as the flame-thrower, turned out to be weapons of considerable value. Others were probably at least as dangerous to the operator as to the intended target.

Most ambitious of all was the Flame Barrage, for setting fire to the beaches and, after some considerable difficulty, even to the sea itself. One or two trials worked under ideal conditions but most failed. Despite this, the Chiefs of Staff (in 1941, after Operation *Sea Lion* had been postponed, though they were not to know it) authorised the construction of these barrages along fifty miles of coastline. The only short sections ever to get completed were at Deal, St Margaret's Bay, the Shakespeare Cliff, Rye and Studland Bay. For many years after the war, the groynes on the beach at Rye were charred and the pebbles above high water coloured pink and white, owing to the high temperatures generated in these experiments. General Brooke was clearly not impressed by the idea of setting the sea alight:

> *This device sounded most promising, but in actual fact was never really successful as it was too dependent on the state of the sea. Even the smallest of waves precluded its use... It was very evident that Lloyd was anxious to 'sell' some of his ideas and to gain credit for his Ministry.* Danchev and Todman, 24 February 1941

Whatever their real efficacy, details of their existence were deliberately leaked, to persuade the German military planners that any invasion force faced a hot welcome. The spoof English-language translations for German troops, produced by Allied propaganda, made particular reference to their prospects of being burnt alive during the invasion. It appears to have worked, insofar as General Loch of the 17th Infantry Division (part of the invasion force) was told by one of his naval advisors, Captain Lehmann, that each port commander in Britain had been issued with fifty motor fire pumps, for the purpose of flooding the sea around their harbour with petrol and setting it alight. Whilst Lehmann was rightly dubious about whether it would work, the Germans nonetheless trained their troops in what to do in such an eventuality. Was this piece of propaganda also, perhaps, the reason for the following invasion story that caught the public eye during the winter of 1940/41?

> *There was a spate of invasion scares that winter (normally the least promising season for sea-borne invasions in these northern waters). In late November, the* News Chronicle *predicted the attack would happen on or around 21 December, on the grounds that 'naval observers point out that there is usually a calm period just before the shortest day of the year.'*

Cooper the Quality Fruiterer offered verse when fruit was in short supply.

The Express had a slightly different take on events. They spoke of 'a widely held view that Hitler may order the Nazi army to make blitz sea raids against us during the long winter nights, and under cover of fog that will envelop the Channel in the coming months.'

But the *Telegraph* in December trumped them all with a report from the United States that the Germans had actually made two unsuccessful invasion attempts and had lost a total of 81,000 troops in the process. According to this masterpiece of invention, the Germans had set out in August 1940 with 60,000 troops in 1,200 specially made aluminium barges. Partway across the Channel, they had come across giant underwater tanks full of petrol, which the Allies had then set alight with incendiary bombs. 'We were caught like fish in a frying pan,' one German soldier is quoted as saying. The French hospitals were said to be full of horribly burned victims. A second attempt, in September, had supposedly led to the same result, and talk of a third had allegedly resulted in widespread mutiny among the armed forces.

Such were Britain's defences in the months following Dunkirk. But what, everyone wondered, were the German plans to overwhelm them? Where were the Germans, and why did they not come?

Chapter Five

Sea Lion

As England, in spite of the hopelessness of her military position, has so far shown herself unwilling to come to any compromise, I have decided to begin to prepare for, and if necessary to carry out, an invasion of England. This operation is dictated by the necessity of eliminating Great Britain as a base from which war with Germany can be fought, and if necessary the island will be occupied. I therefore issue the following orders... Adolf Hitler – opening words of Directive No. 16 – Operation *Sea Lion* (16 July 1940)

The invasion of Britain is an exceptionally daring undertaking, because even if the way is short this is not just a river crossing, but the crossing of sea which is dominated by the enemy... Operational surprise cannot be expected; a defensively prepared and utterly determined enemy face us and dominate the sea which we must use. Adolf Hitler to Admiral Raeder, a private view on Operation *Sea Lion*

A frontal attack against a defence line, on too narrow a front, with no good prospects of surprise, and with insufficient forces reinforced in driblets. Field Marshal Walther von Brauchitsch, describing Operation *Sea Lion*

The early stages of the preparation of Operation *Sea Lion* are, if nothing else, an object lesson in the lack of co-ordination between the three German armed forces. The first work on it was undertaken by Admiral Raeder, probably the least enthusiastic of the three service heads about the whole invasion idea. He could see the enormous logistical and military problems it posed for his own service. He started the work purely as an alibi, something he could produce if questioned by Hitler. On 15 November 1939 he set up a small team, under his Chief of Staff, Vice-Admiral Schniewind, to study the ramifications of an invasion of England. Within five days, they produced a twelve-page document called Study Red. This identified a 60-mile-wide length of coastline for landing between Portland and Yarmouth (Isle of Wight), and their report focussed very much upon the security of the landing fleet, rather than the likely success of the forces, if and when they could be got ashore. It set some stiff pre-conditions for a successful landing:

1. The Royal Navy had to be kept away from the landing area or else destroyed there;
2. The Royal Air Force had to be eliminated;
3. The enemy coastal defences had to be destroyed;
4. Attacks by Royal Navy submarines during the crossing had to be prevented.

In other words, an unopposed landing. The fleet should also embark from German ports since, in their view, even captured foreign ones would be too dangerous. The study was copied to the Armed Forces Supreme Command (OKW) and the army (OKH). The OKH responded with their own proposal, Study Northwest, initiated by Colonel (as he then was) Walther von Brauchitsch. They worked on the assumption that they would have control of the Channel ports and that the bulk of the British Expeditionary Force would be tied down fighting in France. Their point of landing was between the Thames Estuary and The Wash and their objective was to approach London from the north, isolate it and capture it. There was also a diversionary landing planned to the north of the Humber.

Like their navy colleagues, the army planners had some high expectations of their fellow services. The navy, as well as eliminating all sea-borne opposition, from mines to Royal Navy battleships, had to provide fire support for the landing troops, carry out the diversionary landing and prevent the BEF returning from France. Similarly, the Luftwaffe would have to eliminate the RAF, provide attacks on the Royal Navy, carry out airborne landings at Great Yarmouth, Lowestoft and near Cambridge, support the troops as they moved inland and help the navy keep the BEF overseas. They also wanted the landing on a very wide front; General Halder, the German Chief of Staff, at one point described trying to get his men ashore on too narrow a front as being like feeding them through a sausage machine.

The Luftwaffe quickly told the army that their requirements were unachievable: 'The planned deployment is therefore only possible under a condition of total air superiority and even then, only if total surprise is guaranteed.' They added that this 'could only be the final act in an already victorious war against England, otherwise the conditions for the success of such a combined operation would not exist.' Implicit in this we see the Luftwaffe view that it could defeat Britain on its own, which tended to colour Goering's relative lack of interest in *Sea Lion*. The navy was equally dismissive, regarding the army's plans as naive. They had totally ignored the problems of landing the army in such constricted ports and on such difficult beaches. In the event of these landings going ahead, they called upon the army to eliminate coastal defences before the invasion (quite how the army was supposed to do this is not clear). More than anything, there was the problem of the scale of the exercise. The navy in Study Red had envisaged a force of fifteen ships and 7,500 men. The army's plan envisaged 100,000 men and a great deal of heavy equipment crossing the Channel in short order. This, said Schniewind, would require a fleet of some four hundred medium-sized ships (which they did not have) and a large number of sea-going tugboats and barges for landing the troops on the beaches. Moreover, this fleet would need modifying and the whole operation would take a full year to prepare. The one thing all three forces could agree upon was that command of the air was an essential prerequisite for success.

The order for the invasion of the Low Countries (Fuhrer Directive No. 6 Operation *Yellow*) was originally issued on 9 October 1939, but was repeatedly postponed because of bad weather, and bickering among the armed forces. Significantly, no reference was made in the directive to it providing a jumping-off point for an invasion of Britain. This seems not to have been part of Hitler's plans. In the meantime, the Germans carried out a successful sea-borne invasion – of Norway, where the troop-carrying ships simply sailed unopposed into Norwegian ports. But finally, in May 1940, eighty-nine German divisions swept through the Low Countries and into France. The Netherlands fell within five days, Belgium in seventeen, and within about five weeks of launching the attack the Germans were in Paris. With the German forces now on the north French coast, Raeder took it upon himself to raise the matter of invasion with Hitler again, at a meeting with him on 21 May. As before, his motive was to get in before anybody else sold the idea to Hitler, and to spell out the enormous risks and difficulties associated with trying to land an army in Britain. Air supremacy would have to be so complete that it would deter the Royal Navy from trying to interfere with the landings. Hitler listened to his arguments without expressing an opinion and Raeder left the meeting feeling that his case had been well received.

Nonetheless, he still had Rear Admiral Fricke update the earlier Study Red, which re-emerged on 27 May as Study England. This took on board the new military situation and also tried to address some of the criticisms of Study Red made by the army. At the end of May, Raeder even set in motion the first steps towards assembling an invasion fleet, carrying out a detailed audit of all the potentially suitable shipping in Germany and the occupied countries, although he had been given no order or even encouragement from above to do so. He also commissioned a detailed survey of coastal and tidal conditions along the eastern and southern coasts, to help identify suitable landing places. At the same time, the army and the Luftwaffe were also giving some thought to the question of invasion; the Luftwaffe had formed a paratroop division and the army were designing large cross-Channel barges. (Again, all of this was unbidden by any higher authority – at this time, Hitler was convinced that England could be made to sue for peace.) At his 20 June meeting with Hitler, Raeder once more set out the difficulty of invasion across the Channel (as well as complaining about the army designing boats without reference to him) but still received no clear instruction about invasion.

It was at the end of June that General Franz Halder, the Chief of Staff to the army, began to take an active interest in the project. He held detailed discussions with Vice-Admiral Schniewind, who (perhaps foolishly, given the attitude of his superior officer to invasion) gave detailed advice that led Halder towards the opposite conclusion, that invasion was perfectly feasible. Thinking that he had Schniewind's support for a landing between Margate and the Isle of Wight, he set Lieutenant Colonel Pistorius onto developing a new invasion plan. Knowing of Raeder's opposition to the whole scheme, von Brauchitsch gave one of his people the job of solving the cross-Channel transport problem without reference to the navy. Thirteen divisions, over 260,000 well-equipped men, were by now assembled on or near the north French coast. The Luftwaffe also joined in, announcing that they had 25,000 airborne troops (including 6,000-7,000 paratroops) and enough planes and gliders to transport about 16,000 of them in a single attack. Some of these were, however, subsequently diverted to Romania to guard the oil fields. The first indication of any higher approval for all this activity came on 2 July, when the German Forces' Supreme Command gave the instruction to start preparations for invasion on a provisional basis – no date was given and it was to be done 'on the basis that the invasion is still only a plan and has not yet been decided upon.' They were to plan for between 25 and 40 highly mechanised divisions being landed.

Amid all this preparation, Raeder met Hitler again, on 11 July and once more restated the problems associated with a landing. Hitler on this occasion said that his forthcoming speech in the Reichstag would make the British change their minds, and accepted that invasion was very much the last resort. But just two days later, Hitler met with von Brauchitsch and Halder, accepted their plans for invasion without modification, and on 16 July signed the order for *Sea Lion* which gave official blessing to all the planning.

The navy had been given an outline of the army's requirements on 29 June. In summary, they wanted their first wave of thirteen divisions (around 260,000 men) to be landed on a 200-mile front between Ramsgate and Lyme Bay. This front was about five times as long as that later employed by the Allies on D-Day, and left the navy and Luftwaffe with huge problems in defending it. The first wave was to be followed by a second, of unspecified size, to be landed in less than the ten days the navy thought was the minimum time feasible for the task.

There was a fundamental disagreement between the army and the navy. The army were unhappy with the ten-day period for the delivery of the second echelon, while the navy were totally opposed to the scale of the operation and the wide front the army wanted for the crossing, which would be near impossible to protect. As they lacked the surface fleet to defend such a crossing, the German navy saw their only hope as being to create a tightly drawn passage at the narrowest point of the English Channel, hedged in by minefields, submarines and aircraft. The arguments between the services continued right into the detailed preparations. The army wanted the protection of artificial smoke on the beaches, but the navy opposed it, on the grounds that it would increase the (already considerable) risk of the invasion fleet colliding with each other. With the danger of collision also in mind, the (mostly merchant navy) skippers of the invasion fleet also tended to increase the distances between their vessels in the rehearsals; but this made the provision of adequate naval or air protection far more difficult.

But everything hinged upon German air superiority. On 31 July, Admiral Raeder met again with Hitler. They agreed that mid-September was the earliest starting date for the operation and that, if air superiority had not been achieved within a couple of weeks, it should be postponed until the spring of the next year. The Luftwaffe were ordered the next day to begin the destruction of the Royal Air Force.

Meanwhile, the planning – and the arguments – continued. Individual units were sharpening up their landing skills with mock attacks on the French north coast. Goebbels sent a film crew down to capture some of these, and inter-cut it with footage from the Spanish Civil War and the other campaigns of the war so far,

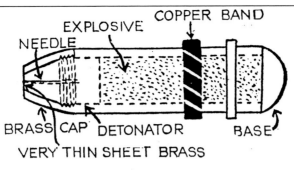

MESSERSCHMITT CANNON SHELLS.

TOO DANGEROUS AS TROPHIES.

The above diagram (in the actual size) is of a Cannon Shell, and is published to show how dangerous they are and to warn the public that they should not be touched. They are fired at close range by Nazi airmen. As they are not balanced for long distance range, there is a tendency for them to land sideways on the earth if they miss their target in the sky. Many have been found in the streets of Dover, and last week when one was picked up by an officer he lost some fingers as a result of it exploding.

They are not much bigger than an ordinary cigar. Their size is 3¼ inches long, and are just over three-quarters of an inch in diameter. The greater portion is lead colour, with a brass nose, and a copper band, which fits the cannon barrel. The tapered point is of very thin brass, and, roughly handled, can easily explode; It is said to be so thin that it can be pierced by a pencil. In this brass end is a needle, which is knocked back by impact into a detonator, which sets off the explosive.

There are two rules to observe when these objects are found : —

(1.) Do not touch, and see that others do not.

(2.) Inform the Police, who will get the proper authorities to deal with it.

No shells, bombs or other missiles that come to earth should be moved.

Living on the front line meant that you were constantly surrounded by dangerous souvenirs of the war.

including Dunkirk, to produce a wholly fictitious – and, as it turned out, highly premature – 'newsreel' of the landings in Britain. Despairing of finding enough vessels to carry the army, the navy requisitioned virtually everything that could float (and some whose buoyancy was questionable). At great disruption to the economy and the war effort, they assembled a fleet of 145 steamers, 1,939 barges, 422 tugs, 944 motorboats and a number of Siebel ferries (an improvised pontoon ferry, designed by an aircraft designer, Fritz Siebel. These were thoroughly disliked by the navy – partly because they had been commissioned by the army, but also because they were very difficult to manoeuvre and were felt to be unstable in all but the calmest of seas).

The barges had a displacement of 500-800, or in some cases 1,300, tons. They were designed to be used on canals and rivers, and even under ideal conditions their seaworthiness was marginal. Very few were self-propelled and the tugs needed to tow them were in short supply. Some of the arrangements for getting them across the Channel were improvised in the extreme. The steamers, in addition to being fully loaded themselves, would be expected to tow two loaded barges. The barges were made even less seaworthy by having collapsible ramps built into the bows, and concrete floors put in them to enable them to carry tanks.

Some of the largest of these could not be towed, but would have to be pushed across the Channel by a couple of minesweepers lashed to the barge's sterns. Crack troops of the *Waffen SS* were to be entrusted to these highly dubious craft, whose crossing of the Channel would, it was estimated, take thirteen hours. With a top speed of 4 knots, these vessels would have been like shooting fish in a barrel for any naval or aerial opposition the Germans failed to subdue, even if they were not first sunk by even a modest swell. At the other extreme, fast launches requisitioned from the customs service would be used to ferry troops ashore. Some would carry advance parties, whose job it would be to clear passages across the beach for the following troops. The army anticipated casualties of 30 to 50 per cent for these units, once ashore.

Landing the essential panzers on the beach was far from straightforward. A number of Panzer IIIs were converted, by waterproofing and the addition of snorkels, to run underwater for short periods. This was not without its problems; seals leaked and, in trials, some crews had to be rescued by divers. On others, the waterproof covering of the eye-slit jammed shut and the panzer would blunder blindly ashore, wrecking everything in its path. Despite having to overcome these difficulties, they had some 250 amphibious tanks ready to go by the middle of September. (These were later used successfully to ford the 13-foot-deep River Bug during the invasion of Russia.)

Some of the other proposals for the invasion force were even more fanciful – none more so than the War Crocodile, designed by Gottfried Feder, an engineer and member of the Nazi Party establishment. This was a giant amphibious tank made of reinforced concrete, some 27 metres long, 6 metres wide and 3.5 metres high, designed to carry 200 men and their equipment, or panzers and other heavy equipment. It would move on tracks while on land and with the help of propellers while at sea, and would (according to some accounts) be capable of creeping across the bed of the English Channel. The idea was actually given serious consideration by the invasion planners, but the huge practical issues it raised could not be resolved in the time available. On a more improvised note, army engineers – more used to building structures for crossing rivers – were sent to scour the coastal areas for anything buoyant that could be strapped to a raft – wine barrels, petrol cans, aircraft drop-tanks, even bags filled with kapok. Very few trials were need to demonstrate how horribly unseaworthy these contraptions were.

If these secret developments were bizarre, those boasted about publicly by the German propaganda services at the time were positively surreal. These talked of dirigible parachutes, which enabled each paratrooper to stay aloft for up to ten hours, concealed as a small cloud by the use of 'fog pills'. They also threatened death rays (and before we scoff at this, it should be remembered that it was from a perfectly serious quest for something similar by the British authorities that the first proposal for radar emerged).

With Teutonic thoroughness, practice runs for loading men and equipment were made as soon as the invasion fleet was assembled. The men and equipment went aboard quite efficiently, but the 60,000 or so horses that were to be the army's main

The day war broke out...

The day war broke out, my missus said to me... she looked at me and she said 'What good are you?'

I said 'Who?'

She said 'You!'

I said, 'How do you mean, what good am I?' 'Well...' she said 'You're too old for the army' she said 'You couldn't get in the navy... and they wouldn't have you in the air force... so what good are you?'... I said 'Don't keep saying what good am I' I said, 'There'll be munitions.' She said 'How can you go on mun...'

I said 'I never said anything about going on munitions, I simply said there'd be some!' 'Well' she said, 'All the young fellas'll be getting called up and you'll have to go back to work!'

Ooh... she's got a cruel tongue! Anyway, I haven't had to go back to work...I'm a lamplighter!...

But the first day I got my [Home Guard] uniform of course, I was very proud of it... I went home and put it on and the Missus looked at me and she said 'What are you supposed to be?'

I said, 'Supposed to... I'm one of the Home Guards.' She said, 'One of the Ho... What are the others like?' She said, 'What are you supposed to do?' I said, 'I'm supposed to stop Hitler's army landing.' She said 'What!... You?'

I said 'No... there's Charlie Evans, Dick Roberts...' I said 'There's seven or eight of us altogether'...

But my Missus, she asks such foolish questions, she said to me, she said 'What are you supposed to be guarding?'

I said, 'We're guarding the British Isles... we're guarding all the men, women and children, millions of 'em... and you!'

She said 'Oh I see... then you're on our side?' I said 'Well of course I am...'

She said 'Well, I think we would stand a far better chance if you were on the other side!'

She said 'Do you know this Hitler?... Have you ever met him?' I said 'Do I... of course I don't!'

She said 'Well how are you going to know which is him if they do land?' I said 'Well, I've got a tongue in my head, haven't I?'

From a Second World War music hall monologue by Robb Wilton

transport proved very unwilling to go aboard or, once aboard, to remain there. One consequence of this was that the cavalry would have faced the indignity of going into battle on bicycles. There were other little loose ends – no provision had been made for dealing with seasickness; this was likely to have been a particular problem for those travelling in the poorly ventilated enclosed barges that were likened to floating coffins.

There were only enough life-jackets for the first wave. These front-line troops were somehow supposed, under battlefield conditions, to return theirs for the use of the following waves. Gas masks were packed away for the trip, not readily accessible to the troops. Given the British plans to drop mustard gas on the invasion beaches, this would have presented a major problem for the troops. It also raises further questions about the state of the horses on arrival. If they were unsettled merely by boarding the vessels, they would no doubt have been thoroughly terrified by the journey, and the bombing and shelling that would have accompanied it. The German troops would then have had to try and get them ashore in an opposed landing including gas attacks.

In August, preparation of the troops even went to the length of the authorities issuing a comprehensive set of guidance documents for the invading forces. One part was a set of maps of the United Kingdom, covering a range of topics from geology to population density. Another provided street plans of the main towns and cities, obtained from the Automobile Association before the war. Another consisted of photographs of views, scenery and famous buildings of Britain, culled from pre-war editions of *The Times*, *Country Life* and *Illustrated London News*. As a tourist guide it was no doubt invaluable, but its use as a military document is not immediately apparent. There was also help for the ordinary soldier, explaining things like the local currency and teaching them useful phrases, both phonetically and in the correct spelling. The British spoofed this latter in leaflet drops, offering them translations of such essential pieces of conversation as, 'We are seasick – where is the basin?', 'See how briskly our captain burns!' (this latter to reinforce British propaganda about their 'secret' weapons to set the sea ablaze) and 'Why is the Fuhrer not coming with us?'. The official guidance went largely unread as the delays lengthened, and the reading of any British alternatives was strictly forbidden to the German troops.

The final plan of attack

The final version of *Sea Lion* envisaged five broad routes for the crossing:

> from Ostende to the area between Deal and Ramsgate; from Dunkirk and Calais to the area between Folkestone and Dungeness; from Calais to the area between Dungeness and Cliff End; from Boulogne to the area between Pevensey and Beachy Head, and from Le Havre to the area between Brighton and Selsey Bill.

A total of nine divisions from the Ninth and Sixteenth armies would make the landings, supported by four battalions of light and medium tanks. There would also be aerial drops by 7th Flieger Division, whose task it would be to take the high ground north and north-west of Folkestone, secure crossings of the Royal Military Canal for the sea-borne troops and place a roadblock on the Canterbury-Folkestone road. Other airborne troops would be landed on the towns behind Brighton. A substantial bridgehead should be established by the fifth day. It was estimated that it would take the British this long to counter-attack in strength, given the Luftwaffe's anticipated mastery of the skies and their consequent ability to harass the advancing forces and destroy bridges and other key parts of the route. The Sixteenth Army would form up on the line between Canterbury, Ashford, Tenterden and Etchingham, whilst the Ninth Army would aim to control a line from 'the high ground 29km north and west of Bexhill' through Uckfield to 'the high ground west and south-west of Lewes'. From there, they were to break out to take their first objective, a line between Portsmouth, Petersfield, Reigate and Gravesend.

The original plans for *Sea Lion* also had the Sixth Army crossing from

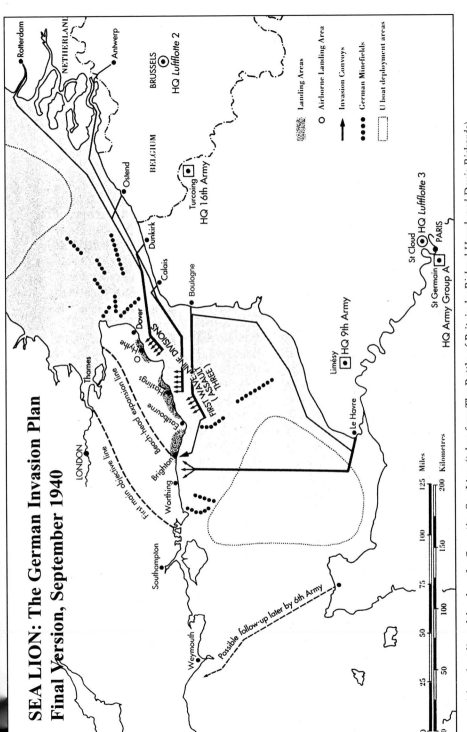

A broad outline of the plans for Operation Sea Lion (*taken from* The Battle of Britain *by Richard Hough and Denis Richards*).

Cherbourg to Lyme Bay, and from there performing a wide encircling movement to the west and north of London, but this was not included in the final version.

An early priority was to secure an airfield in the bridgehead and Lympne was the chosen target. It became the objective of airborne troops from 7th Flieger and the 22nd Air Landing divisions. Two minutes after dawn on the day of the invasion, the first waves were to be dropped, near Hythe and around Paddlesworth and Etchinghill. Both were to make their way to Sandgate, where Stukas would be sent in to deal with heavy artillery spotted there. The troop-carrying planes would return to France and collect the second wave, to be dropped around Sellinge and Postling. Together, the two waves would surround the airfield, following which a third wave would reinforce them and consolidate their hold on the area. There would then be a combined ground and glider attack, on the airfield and subsequently on the higher ground beyond it. Once the airfield was secured, 22nd Division could be flown in, a wider area occupied and the first advance fighter units brought in.

Lucas, who built up this sequence of events from a German plan now held by the Imperial War Museum, doubts whether the units concerned had the capability to undertake this demanding operation. They had been seriously weakened in the

May 1940, and a solitary private of the Royal West Kents stands guard on the cliffs near Dover. The trouble was, on some stretches of exposed coast that was almost all there was.

fighting on continental Europe and he questions whether their replacements had been sufficiently trained. They were also short of planes and almost every other kind of equipment. In addition, the airborne forces at that time had no way of dropping in heavier artillery. Among the troops opposing them would have been the 7th Lyminge Battalion of the Home Guard, who covered the area from just inland of Folkestone down to Romney Marsh. James Lucas. *Storming Eagles: German Airborne Forces in World War 2*, Cassell, 1988, pp. 57-63

The initial landing would not have been nine full divisions, but a first wave of 6,700 from each, totalling some 60,300 men – little more than three full divisions. These would initially have formed three separate areas of beachheads, with:

26,800 seeking to land between Folkestone and St Leonards; 13,400 between Bexhill and Eastbourne, and 20,100 between Beachy Head and Brighton.

They would have had 250 tanks, but little other artillery. Even this presupposes that all the men and equipment would get ashore safely and in the right place – a huge speculation, given the complexity of the operation and the haphazard nature of the invasion fleet, with vessels of vastly differing speed, manoeuvrability and seaworthiness. The OKH operational order for *Sea Lion* said at one point:

Commanders and troops must realise that the peculiar conditions of sea transport render the disintegration of formations inevitable. Fleming, p. 257

This was true even before account is taken of the effect of naval and air attacks, and of shelling from the heavy artillery on the coast. Add to this whatever toll would be taken of them during the landings themselves (bearing in mind the 30 to 50 per cent casualties anticipated among some of their advance troops) and the total numbers initially coming off the beaches might have been substantially less than three full divisions. The plan for reinforcement envisaged them arriving at a maximum of two divisions a day, although it would have taken a total of eleven days to get the entire force to England. These reinforcements could themselves have been subject to much the same rate of attrition as the first wave.

Over and above these, there were elaborate decoy plans for invasions in the areas between Edinburgh and Newcastle, The Wash and Harwich, and Wexford and Dungarvan in Eire. The German propaganda machine was to be used to give credence to these, though the German navy did not have sufficient spare shipping to give them a convincing physical presence.

The navy still regarded this shopping list with horror. They calculated that the first wave alone – even if they left behind most of the anti-aircraft guns – would require 45 transport ships, 640 barges, 215 tugs and 550 motorboats, not to mention the full facilities of every port from Ostend to Cherbourg. Moving the second echelons in one go would have required some 2 million tons of shipping – more than the Germans had (or could acquire) and, more to the point, more than would fit into the embarkation ports. Even spreading the second echelon over ten days, the fleet required would take them until at least mid-September to assemble, and the first suitable period for landing after that would be in late September, when good

The bells! The bells!

From 13 June 1940, there was even a ban on the ringing of church bells, except in the event of an invasion. *Ringing World*, the journal of the campanologists, was outraged:

> *a stunning blow to ringing, from which, even when the war is over, it will take a long time to recover.* Fleming, p. 96

For good measure, they pointed out that anyone attempting to ring bells without proper training either might not be able to make them work, or could do themselves a nasty injury. After the great false alarm of 7 September, doubts began to grow about the efficacy of this form of communication. It was pointed out in Parliament that the people missed the sound of bells, that the church was inevitably the one building without a telephone, and that the use of churches for a military purpose might attract reprisals from the enemy. The ban on the ringing of church bells was finally lifted on 4 April 1943. As Churchill wryly observed, 'For myself, I cannot help feeling that anything like a serious invasion would be bound to leak out!'

weather was far from guaranteed. As early as July, the navy was recommending postponement until the spring of 1941, but they were ordered to continue (not least in hopes of intimidating the British into submission in the meantime).

For his part, General Halder, on hearing the navy's timescale for completing the crossings, said: 'All previous statements of the navy were so much rubbish and we can throw away the whole plan of an invasion.'

Collier outlines the overall initial objectives for the invasion force:

> *The initial task assigned to General Busch was to take Dover and advance at least as far as a line extended from the heights between Canterbury and Folkestone through Ashford to the neighbourhood of Hawkhurst. Meanwhile General Straus was to advance towards a line from Hadlow Down to the high ground west of Lewes. Between them the two armies would thus occupy a bridgehead about fifteen miles deep from the middle of east Kent to the northern escarpment of the South Downs north of Brighton. 'After the arrival of sufficient forces on British soil,' ran the instruction signed by Field-Marshal von Brauchitsch, 'the army group will attack and secure possession of the line Thames Estuary-heights south of London-Portsmouth. As soon as the situation permits, mobile formations will be pushed forward to the area west of London in order to cut off London from the south and west and to capture crossings over the Thames for an advance in the direction of Watford-Swindon'.* Collier, p. 178

Kieser gives us an example of the more detailed plans for one of those first divisions. The 17th Infantry Division of the Sixteenth Army, under General Loch, had been assigned part of the sector between Hythe and Dymchurch, next to 35th Division and supported by paratroops. In front of the village of Dymchurch ran the Dymchurch Wall, a sea defence wall, running for several miles with few and narrow access points. Some of these could be covered by gunfire from two nearby Martello towers. The Luftwaffe was supposed to eliminate these towers beforehand; if they failed to do so, the towers would be the troops' first target. Beyond the beach there was the further obstacle of that other defensive barrier from Napoleonic times, the Royal Military Canal. If they got past that, they faced a marshy area with few roads and few settlements that might double as bases for the troops.

They were supposed to live off the land as far as possible during those first few weeks, to minimise the amount of supplies that had to be shipped in. But this isolated, thinly populated area did not hold out promising prospects for doing so. Even the 125,000 sheep which used to graze there had been evacuated to safer fields in the Home Counties. The local population had had it drummed into them not to make food, fuel or other essentials available to the enemy. But most of them were already gone, moved out in May to allow troops to be billeted in the holiday camps along the Dungeness peninsula and to train in the marshes. The narrow-gauge Romney, Hythe and Dymchurch Railway, which before the war had taken tourists on pleasure trips along the coast, had been requisitioned and became a troop carrier. An armoured train, mounted with Lewis guns and an anti-tank rifle, was stationed just to the east of Dymchurch.

The plan was to put ashore 1,250 infantrymen from each regiment as a first wave, along with engineers armed with flame-throwers and rocket launchers, light artillery and communications. Their first-day objective was to reach the high ground beyond the Military Canal, about 3 miles inland. The Germans knew from their monitoring of British military signals traffic that the bulk of the British forces were based some 60 miles inland, and they hoped to secure the initial bridgehead with relatively light casualties. Once they were established, and reinforced by successive waves, they were to advance north-east to Dover and north to Ashford.

The sea defences at Dymchurch would have been one of the first obstacles facing the amphibious panzers, if and when they got ashore.

A large, well-kept secret

In the summer of 1940, when things looked their worst, an acquaintance of mine, then an officer of long service who had, in the dim past, been trained on railroad guns, was despatched with a companion to reconnoitre likely sites on the coast of England to which the few available railroad guns could be sent. Having studied the map, they came to the conclusion that a little valley near a main rail line would be suitable, providing a short spur of track could be laid into it, and they set out to study the ground. Walking through a wood, they were surprised to find a rusty single-track spur leading right towards their selected valley, though not shown on the map. Pleased with their good fortune, they followed the tracks into the valley, where the rails disappeared into two weather-beaten sheds. Peering through the cobwebbed windows, they discerned, dimly, what appeared to be some form of machinery. Feeling that here was a fine place to park a pair of guns, they broke a lock on the door and entered the gloom. Before them was a gleaming 9.2-inch railroad gun; the other shed proved to hold another one. At this point, they were disturbed by a posse of police and troops, alerted by a suspicious shepherd – people were very touchy at that time and place – and with them came an elderly pensioner who turned out to be the caretaker of the two guns. Yes, they were fully serviceable; yes, they'd been there since 1918 and he was paid every week through the Post Office to keep them clean and greased, and so he had, and bless me, sir, d'you tell me as you didn't know they was there?

Well, it's a nice story; and anything could happen in England in 1940.

Ian V Hogg. The Guns 1939-45, (Ballantyne, New York, 1970) p. 120

Among the other forces travelling from Dunkirk were members of the 1st Battalion Brandenburg Commandos. Part of the battalion was to destroy the locks at Folkestone in an airborne operation. The rest were to make their way to Dungeness and destroy the railway guns there, which might otherwise be used against further waves of the invasion fleet. Their secondary targets were the area's locks and power plants. Their 3rd Battalion, travelling from Caen, was being used to capture Weymouth in a diversionary attack. The purpose of this was to draw British forces away from Portsmouth and Plymouth, where more major attacks were planned.

Meanwhile, other preparations were making good progress. The German army stationed all the troops involved in the first wave either at the coast or close to it. Special training had started by the end of July. Even the third and fourth waves were aiming to be battle-ready and in a position to embark by late September. The invasion fleet was steadily being assembled. About a third of the tonnage they needed was requisitioned from the Low Countries; the remainder would have to be diverted from meeting the needs of the German economy – about a third of the German merchant fleet, all their trawlers and almost all their large tugs. It would be a major disruption to the German economy. The scale of, and priority given to, these preparations can hardly be overstated. U-boat construction and the completion of the battleship *Tirpitz* were both delayed. Giant cranes had to be brought from Germany to help repair the embarkation ports and the locks and canals that served them. Some 20,000 seamen were needed for the operation. Every available naval reserve was called up, and any members of the other services with marine experience were transferred across to it. Large numbers of merchant seamen were also requisitioned.

The main ingredient that was missing was air supremacy. The first suitable day for invasion was thought to be 21 September, which meant that Hitler would have had to give the order for invasion by 11 September, in turn giving Goering his deadline for securing mastery of the air. First Hitler postponed the decision until the 14th. On the 13th Admiral Halder told Hitler that Goering had failed to provide the conditions the navy needed to make the crossing. Hitler then postponed a decision again until the 17th, making the earliest possible start date 27 September. If they did not go that day, the moon and tides would not be favourable again until 8 October, by which time the weather would be much more uncertain.

But meanwhile Bomber Command was starting to have a significant impact on the invasion fleet. Their attacks showed the value of radar, in the negative sense that the Germans did not have it and their fighters would often arrive too late to intervene. By 21 September, some 21 steamers, 194 barges and numerous other vessels – over a tenth of the fleet – had been lost or damaged by bombing, along with vast quantities of munitions. (So brightly were the occupied Channel ports blazing that the British pilots nicknamed these raids 'The Blackpool Run', after the illuminations.) There were no reserves of ships to replace them – the barrel had been well and truly scraped. Hitler had to order the fleet to be dispersed to protect it from further damage.

This was the beginning of the end for any invasion plans in 1940, although they were only formally abandoned for the year on 12 October. Some of the vessels were returned to their original use. Others had been so cannibalised that they were no longer good for any other purpose. Key personnel were also redeployed. Initially,

---

Good news about bombing
From the *Sussex Daily News*, 1 September 1939. As the shadow of war fell over the nation, the authorities had some cheery news about the effects of bombing:

It should be borne in mind that the direct effects of a high-explosive bomb, that is, the effects that cause major destruction, extend over a very limited range, not further in most cases than a thirty foot circle round the bomb.

It may be assumed that if as many as fifty bombs of the largest size fell in a square mile, any individual within that square mile would have something like a hundred-to-one chance of escaping what may be called the 'direct hit effects'. [Author: I think – hope – they meant a hundred-to-one chance of being hit.]

It is the secondary effects, that is, splinters – including splinters of shells from anti-aircraft guns – blast and the fall of debris which are liable to cause by far the greatest number of casualties, and the individual can do a great deal to protect himself against such effects... People should not be upset by pictures of what happened to the poorly-built houses in Spain.

the operation was merely postponed until the following spring or summer, but the lead-in time for reactivating it grew longer and longer, as the logistical problems involved became better understood by the navy, in particular. It started out at thirty days, increased to forty-five by December 1940, and to two months by the following March (plus six months for the construction of new barges – the navy were by then working on a new design of barge that could carry three panzers at 13-15 knots). There were still those, like Halder, who continued to see it as a realistic possibility, even to the extent of regarding Hitler's invasion of Russia as a gigantic feint, designed to mislead the British. But Hitler, according to Collier, had long since abandoned it as a serious prospect:

> *Hitler... considered the British Army, in view of its slow rate of expansion, brief experience of modern warfare and heavy losses of equipment in northern France, would be capable of little in 1940, but would be formidable by the spring. In short, he believed that if a landing was to be made at all, it had best be done before the winter.* Collier, p. 181

Even so, substantial numbers of troops were held in a permanent state of semi-readiness in northern France, long after it had ceased to be a remotely realistic proposition. A revised version of *Sea Lion*, called Operation *Shark*, was still being worked on in April 1941. Only in February 1944, six months before the Allies' own D-Day, did the German navy formally discontinue construction work for invasion.

But before the threat of invasion could be removed, Britain – and in particular, its air force – had to face its greatest challenge.

Chapter Six

The Few... and the Many

Personally I always felt that if we won the Battle of Britain the Germans would not invade, and that if we lost it they would have no need to invade... the Luftwaffe could have proceeded to wipe out in their own time and without any significant hindrance, first our air stations, then our aircraft factories, then perhaps our other munitions factories, then our ports and so on. The point would have been reached, perhaps quite soon, when we would have been bereft of all means of serious opposition... General Ismay, Chief of Staff to Winston Churchill

When you are driving, you don't hear much of what goes on outside and sometimes you get a bit of a shock when you find a 'yellow-nose' flying along beside you, during the daytime, and the run anywhere between Folkestone, Dover and Deal can be quite lively. It was not just Spitfire pilots who had close encounters with Messerschmitts. This was an east Kent bus driver, quoted in H R P Boorman. *Hell's Corner 1940, Kent Messenger,* 1942

The Few – the Battle of Britain

The one thing all the German armed forces agreed upon was that control of the airspace over south-east England was an essential prerequisite to invasion. Once France had been conquered, Goering and the Luftwaffe turned their attention to the Royal Air Force.

Overall control of RAF Fighter Command was exercised from Stanmore Park, to the north of London. They were organised into areas or groups; 11 Group covered the south-east from its operations room, 100 feet underground at Uxbridge, 15 miles to the west of London. The groups in turn were sub-divided into sectors, each with its main sector airfield. The sectors covering Kent and Sussex were based on Tangmere, Kenley, Biggin Hill and Hornchurch. The sector stations themselves had satellite stations and advanced landing fields, and there were also airfields in the area used by Coastal Command and other units less directly critical to the control of British airspace.

The battle started in the first half of July, with German attacks on British convoys passing through the English Channel. These were designed partly to do damage to the British economy, partly to train Luftwaffe pilots in bomber-fighter co-operation, but mostly to lure Fighter Command out into large-scale battles, which the Luftwaffe believed they could win. They thought that even an equal rate of losses would see the RAF exhausted first.

The first real day of the battle, 10 July, saw a dogfight of over a hundred aircraft above the Channel. From the start, there were ominous warnings for the Luftwaffe. Over the first two days of the fighting, German losses were thirty-three to the British ten. But, for the most part, Dowding, the Air Chief Marshal of Fighter Command, refused to allow large numbers of fighters onto convoy escort, concentrating their main efforts on attacking German bombers. One consequence

Pilots of 32 Squadron at Hawkinge grab a moment's relaxation near to their Hurricanes, before the next scramble.

of this was the loss of 30,000 tons of shipping between 10 July and 12 August (out of 5 million tons passing round those coasts). The Government's tough decision was that it was easier to replace coastal shipping than fighter aircraft, if the choice had to be made. Their other response was to minimise the number of convoys passing through the Strait, leading among other things to severe congestion in the west-coast ports.

On 19 July, the Luftwaffe attacked Dover harbour, where 120 Stukas and Bf109s sank a 12,000-ton Royal Navy tanker, the *War Sepoy*. Later in July, the Germans ordered a halt to the bombing of south-coast port facilities, on the grounds that they would need them undamaged for the invasion. Five days later, they sank five ships totalling 17,000 tons and severely damaged six more. From then, merchant shipping only passed through the Strait at night.

Hitler grew impatient with the rate of progress in gaining air superiority. On 1 August, he issued Directive No. 17 to the Luftwaffe, ordering them to 'overpower the English air force with all the forces at their command, in the shortest possible time.' Goering named 10 August as his *Adlertag* (Eagle Day), when the all-out onslaught would begin, and set out a two-week timetable for securing German command of the air. In the event, suitable weather conditions did not materialise until 12 August, when the Luftwaffe launched heavy raids on the airfields at Manston, Hawkinge and Lympne, and the radar stations at Dover, Rye, Dunkirk and Ventnor. Of the latter, Ventnor suffered particularly serious damage and was not fully operational for months afterwards. Had they persisted with their attacks on the radar stations, the results could have been near fatal to the ability of the RAF to fight the battle. However, Goering ordered on 19 August that there were to be no more attacks on them. (There was in fact just one further attack, on 31 August).

This was one of the decisions on which the Battle of Britain turned. Over the following weeks, the RAF stations in Kent and Sussex (and elsewhere) were repeatedly attacked and seriously damaged. August and the early part of September was the most testing time for Fighter Command. Repeated bombing of their airfields taxed even their capacity to patch them up. By the end of August, Manston was inoperative, West Malling, Lympne and Hawkinge were hanging on by a thread, Biggin Hill was badly damaged and operating at below capacity, with its operations room in a cobbler's shop in the village, and Kenley was being run from Spice and Wallis's butcher's shop in Caterham High Street. The Germans only had to finish off these, plus Tangmere, Croydon and Gravesend and there would have been no serviceable fighter airfield between them and London.

Fighter Command was losing ground. In addition to the damage to airfields, the loss of planes, and more particularly of the pilots to fly them, was taking place faster than they could be replaced. On these trends, it seemed only a matter of time before the Germans gained control of the skies over England. What Fighter Command desperately needed was a period of retrenchment.

Wartime fund-raising: Here, a Messerschmidt Bf109 (former property of a Herr Raisinger) goes on display in the Rootes Group showroom in Maidstone.

Sir Keith Park, Head of 11 Group, Fighter Command, said of this period:

The enemy's bombing attacks by day did extensive damage to five of our forward aerodromes and also to six of our seven sector stations. There was a critical period when the damage to sector stations and our ground organisations was having a serious effect on the fighting efficiency of the squadrons. Richard Hough and Denis Richards. *The Battle of Britain,* Hodder and Stoughton, 1989, p. 236

There were also serious attacks on the main aircraft factories, threatening future supplies to Fighter Command. But in one of these attacks, on 24 August, some of the planes overshot the Short Brothers' factory in Rochester and dropped their bombs on central London instead. This prompted Churchill to order a retaliatory attack on Berlin for the following night. Its effects were minimal, but the loss of face for Hitler and Goering was out of all proportion, especially when it was followed up by further attacks the following night. This led at first to a redoubling of effort by the Luftwaffe in their attacks on the airfields, with senior officers within the Luftwaffe claiming on 29 August that unlimited fighter superiority had been achieved. The fact that they lost thirty-six planes the following day may have given them cause to reconsider this.

But from 7 September, on Hitler's orders, London became the principal target. The thinking behind this appears to have been partly revenge for the Berlin attacks, and partly a belief that a concentrated attack on the capital city would so sap the morale of the civilian population that the Government would be forced to sue for peace. It was also thought that this would finally lure the remains of Fighter Command out for the major confrontation that Goering had sought from the outset. This was another critical decision for the Battle of Britain. Dreadful though its consequences for the civilian population were, it gave Fighter Command precious time to repair its airfields, and get more planes and pilots into operation. Goering finally got his big battle, on 15 September, the day subsequently commemorated as Battle of Britain Day. The largest numbers of German planes ever seen over London and the south-east were met by twenty-four RAF squadrons, with the result that the Germans lost sixty planes against twenty-four RAF fighters.

The raids continued on into September, but major urban areas and aircraft factories, rather than RAF airfields, remained the main targets. Large-scale daylight bombing ended on 30 September, when raids on London and Yeovil cost the Germans forty-eight planes in return for achieving very little damage. The final phase saw opportunistic fighter-bomber raids by day and larger-scale bombing of cities by night. The Battle of Britain effectively came to a close by the end of October and, with it, any immediate prospect of invasion.

Why did the Germans fail? Apart from the crucial decisions not to persist with their attacks on the radar and the airfields, and to turn their attention instead to London, their strategy was based upon bad intelligence about their enemy in almost every particular. They had an approximately correct estimate of the initial strength of Fighter Command, but got virtually everything else wrong.

First, they greatly underestimated the rate at which the British, under their new

Some front-line towns – Air-raid deaths

Town	Air-raid deaths
Dover (including rural district)	204
Brighton	198
Eastbourne	174
Hastings and St Leonards	154
Dartford (including rural district)	142
Canterbury	115
Ashford	103
Folkestone	85
Sevenoaks (including rural district)	84
Ramsgate	84
Rochester	75
Maidstone (including rural district)	69
Deal	64
Swanscombe	62
Gillingham	57
Chatham	47
Malling	46
Northfleet	40
Gravesend	38
Margate	35

Sources: Rootes p. 200; *Sussex Express and County Herald*. Figures do not include East Grinstead, which suffered 108 deaths in a single raid.

Minister of Aircraft Production, Lord Beaverbrook, could replace lost fighters. They underestimated the performance of both Spitfires and Hurricanes (not least since, around the time of the fall of France, the British planes switched from 87-octane to 100-octane petrol, obtained in great secrecy from the American Esso company, to give a significant boost in performance. This was initially denied to the British by the American Government under the Neutrality Act. The Germans did not find out about it until late August). They correspondingly overestimated the capabilities of their twin-engined Messerschmitt 110 fighter and Junkers 87 dive-bomber. The former were so outclassed by the RAF that they themselves required fighter protection and the latter became known as 'flying coffins' and had to be withdrawn. Their single-engined Messerschmitt Bf109 was superior in most respects to the Hurricane and the approximate equal of the Spitfire, but was bedevilled by its limited range, particularly when escorting bombers (for which it was not well suited). Under these circumstances, it could not provide cover for bombers beyond the north-west corner of London. Many Bf109s survived missions over England, only to ditch in the Channel from lack of fuel. The Spitfire's range was, if anything, worse than the Bf109's, but this was less of an issue since they were playing at home. Finally, their bombers were ill-suited to the role they were asked to perform, of long-range strategic bombing against fixed targets in a situation where they were opposed in the air. They were designed more for close support of the army in a mobile war, preferably where the opposing air force had been neutralised.

They had poor intelligence about the location of the Allied fighter airfields, with the result that significant effort was expended on airfields used by Coastal Command and other less crucial units. They were doubtful about the very existence of Allied radar, and certainly underestimated the importance of it and its associated command structures. They (in particular Kesselring, the Head of the Luftwaffe under Goering) also greatly overestimated the destructive effects of their raids. They would tend to assume that any airfield they had bombed (and the aircraft operating from it) could be written out of the equation. In practice, RAF crews could often get even a badly bombed grass airfield back into operational use within hours, and the loss of airfield buildings was more inconvenient than paralysing. (In fact, the commanding officer at Biggin Hill actually blew up the last of his hangars himself, in an effort to convince German intelligence that his airfield was no longer operational.) The Germans frequently had to re-bomb airfields they had previously written off. Damage to airfield communications with the centre was quite another matter.

Personnel matters were also on the British side. Any German pilot brought down over Britain became a prisoner of war, whereas an RAF pilot who baled out safely over Kent or Sussex could be airborne again next day. Over the Channel, the Germans' air-sea rescue arrangements were rather better developed than the British ones. Given the tendency of their Bf109s to end up in the Channel, they needed to be.

On the ground

But what of its effects on the people watching this spectacle from below? As the Battle of Britain got under way, Dover became the headquarters of a posse of international reporters covering the conflict. This group, some forty in number, evidently overwhelmed the local telecommunications network, since they lobbied successfully for it to be upgraded to cope with the increased volume of calls. Among them was a young BBC reporter, Charles Gardner, who travelled about wearing a tin helmet and with a mattress strapped to the roof of his car for protection. He it was who made one of the most famous (some would say infamous) broadcasts of the war, an account of a dogfight over Dover, making the proceedings sound to some ears uncomfortably like the commentary to a sporting event. An extract will give the flavour:

> There is a dogfight up there... there are two, three, four machines, they're circling. Watch out! Machine gun fire! Watch out! One, two, three, four, five, six... and now they've gone. Yes! They're being chased, and how they are chasing them home: three Spitfires are after three Messerschmitts. Oh boy! Just look at that! How the Messerschmitts... Oh, this is really fantastic... and one Spitfire after the one in front... He's got them!

More fund-raising, this time for Warship Week in February 1942. Here, the ladies of Canterbury portray 'Girls of the Empire's Allies'.

With so much of the battle taking place over their heads, it was no surprise that Kent and Sussex towns became enthusiastic supporters of the collections for Spitfires. Hastings launched theirs in August 1940, with Alderman A Blackman promising the first £1,000 if the town could raise the remaining £4,000 inside a month. The town briefly went Spitfire mad, with sales of goods, the manufacture of Spitfire golliwogs, shop-window displays, and fines for darts players at the Cambridge Hotel scoring less than ten. Almost any piece of German memorabilia went on display for an admission charge. Residents paid good money to see a single German parachute at White Rock. At the other extreme, a Heinkel bomber, shot down 'but in remarkably good condition' attracted the crowds at Summer Fields. But there was always someone who did not get the point. One man, asked to buy a raffle ticket for the Spitfire, declined on the grounds that he would not know what to do with it if he won it. But the prize for the most ingenious raffle went to one organised by the Red Cross, which raised £3 from a single banana. For the benefit of younger readers who might not remember them, the newspaper explained that it was 'an elongated yellow tropical or sub-tropical fruit'.

Right from the start of hostilities, people were warned of the dangers of standing outside to watch the dogfights in the skies above. The *Kent Messenger* carried whole columns of stories of injuries and near-misses from shrapnel. Not even the Deputy Town Clerk of Dover, William Ransome, could resist going out to watch a dogfight, as he recalled:

> *I was just turning to go in when I felt what I thought was a sandbag fall on my shoulder. I thought my neighbour was having some fun with me, until I put my hand behind me and felt blood.*
>
> *At the time I was by myself, so I called over to my neighbour and asked him to come in, because I had been hit.*
>
> *He came in and said 'By jingo, you'll have to go to the doctor; there's a hole in your back'.* Boorman, p. 113

More serious threats faced those living near searchlight and anti-aircraft gun emplacements, or more particularly near airfields, who faced the threat of German raids spilling over onto them. A raid on Hawkinge on 7 September ended with a shelter in the village being bombed, killing six civilians. Ramsgate suffered even higher casualties on 24 August, when the second wave of an attack on nearby Manston turned instead on the town. Thirty-one people were killed, forty-five injured and 1,200 houses destroyed in the raid.

Sometimes the civilian population would find RAF pilots either force-landing or parachuting down among them. Often the pilots would be treated as heroes. One team, sent to recover a Hurricane pilot who had force-landed in a field near Sittingbourne, found him sitting in the middle of the field in a large armchair supplied by the local residents, his feet resting on two crates of brown ale donated by the village pub, and eating plates of sandwiches. It was not unknown for downed pilots to be so well-plied with alcohol by their rescuers that they did not need any anaesthetic when they went to hospital to have their wounds treated. But few pilots can have shown greater resourcefulness than Flying Officer Jimmy Coward. His foot was shot off by a cannon shell and he baled out. During his descent, he fashioned a tourniquet for his leg from the radio leads on his flying helmet and survived the landing.

But occasionally, they could be the victim of class prejudice and worse. Pilot Officer Kenneth Lee recounts the experience of being shot down and slightly wounded:

> *I was taken to a local golf club, just inland from Whitstable, to await an ambulance. I was in shirtsleeves, slightly bloodstained, but couldn't help hearing members at the last hole complaining that the distraction of the battle in the air was disturbing their putting, whilst once inside a voice demanded, 'Who's that scruffy-looking chap at the bar? I don't think he's a member.'* Hough and Richards, p. 211

But this was nothing to the fate that befell Flight Lieutenant James Nicholson. His Hurricane caught fire and he was wounded twice by cannon shells but, before baling out, he managed to shoot down an enemy fighter, an act that won him the only Victoria Cross of the Battle of Britain. When he finally landed, badly burned and seriously injured, he was shot again by an over-zealous Home Guard who thought he was a German.

Kent towns were among the most enthusiastic supporters of the Spitfire funds, and eventually paid for an entire squadron of planes.

... and the Battle for Europe

As autumn 1940 moved towards winter, some thought the danger of invasion was receding, at least for the moment. For others, winter fogs, accompanied as they usually were by calm seas, represented one of the most dangerous times for invasion. But by the end of October, the Government decided that the threat of a major invasion in the next five months could be discounted in most areas. Only in the area between North Foreland and Dungeness was it felt that a significant landing might be made from self-propelled barges. Two field divisions were kept in Kent against this eventuality and the remainder were withdrawn for urgently needed training and re-equipping. The beaches were to be guarded by lower-order troops, with little artillery or transport.

The winter's training was a comprehensive and demanding exercise in mobile warfare. Troops were thrown into simulated battle situations directly after completing forced marches of up to 40 miles, or 200 miles in vehicles. Routes were planned to cover every eventuality and arrangements for managing both military traffic and the flow of refugees were put in place. The command structures were also reviewed and Eastern Command (which covered the whole area from The Wash to west of Portsmouth) was split in two. The new South-Eastern Command took over all the area south of the Thames. South-east England was putting itself on a proper war footing, just as the German interest in invasion was starting to recede.

By 1943 the threat of German invasion was effectively over and the Allies' own plans for invasion were beginning to form. Kent and Sussex played a large part in these, but no invasion was launched across that part of the Channel – the area was used for a range of decoys. The first, in September 1943, was Operation *Starkey*, designed to simulate a large-scale landing in the Pas-de-Calais. Its real purpose was to concentrate German troops in the north of France as the Allies invaded Italy on 3 September, though it was also a useful dummy run for the logistics of D-Day, the following year. Large-scale convoys were moved around the area, non-essential personnel were banned from the area and a modest 'invasion fleet' sailed to within a few miles of the French coast.

The following year saw activity on a much larger scale, as the real invasion plans were finalised. From 1 April 1944, a coastal area 10 miles deep from Lincolnshire to Land's End was closed to all but residents and the 1,421,000 members of the Allied forces who were stationed in Britain by that spring. The south-east corner of England became the scene of a deception on a vast scale to persuade the Germans that the Allies planned the mirror-image of Operation *Sea Lion*. A huge mock-up of an oil dock and pumping head was constructed at Dover by staff from the film and stage industry. Elaborate arrangements were made to persuade the world that they were genuine – the King and Montgomery inspected them and the RAF protected them. Roads were constructed across all the most suitable beaches along the coast and were lit at night to suggest loading was going on.

Vast numbers of troops and military materials were moved about the area, often bringing towns to a highly visible gridlock. New roads and bridges were built, the entrances to coastal towns were guarded and everything was done to suggest the (not-too-well-hidden) secret preparations for invasion. About 400 dummy landing craft were assembled in the coastal ports from Lowestoft to Folkestone. Guns and heavy armour – all made of inflatable rubber – were parked in fields, and signs were erected to suggest to any passing fifth columnist that the invasion was due to start from there, about six weeks after the date of Operation *Overlord*. Advance landing grounds across the south-east created the illusion that there were fifty squadrons based in Kent alone.

Other elaborate measures were taken to persuade the Germans that Dover was

It looks like a seaside bungalow at Greatstone, but is in fact one of thirty-four pumping-houses for the PLUTO cross-Channel pipeline, which supplied petrol to the Allied forces in Normandy after D-Day.

in fact the real headquarters for the preparation of D-Day (and, by inference, that the invasion fleet would cross the Dover Strait). Montgomery's radio traffic from Portsmouth was sent by cable to Dover, from where it was transmitted, to give the illusion that his headquarters were there. They even created a fictitious army group – FUSAG, the First United States Army Group – with enough radio traffic and other activity to persuade the Germans of their existence. German spies who had been turned by the British sent back intelligence to confirm this non-existent build-up of forces. So successful was the deception that, even after the Normandy landings were under way, the Germans still thought they were nothing more than a feint for the bigger landing that was coming in the Pas-de-Calais.

On 6 June 1944, the Allies returned to France. But the south-east corner of England still faced the final trial of the V-weapons (*Vergeltung*, for revenge) fired from France and the Low Countries. A total of 1,422 V1s came down in Kent alone, killing 150 people and injuring 1,716 others. As described earlier, the defence forces responded quickly, using fighters, barrage balloons and a solid line of anti-aircraft guns across the North Downs. Sixty-four of the V2 rockets – against which there was no defence – also landed in Kent. Only as the Allied forces advanced far enough to capture the launching sites for Hitler's V-weapons and the heavy gun emplacements on the French coast (the last of the latter fell on 30 September 1944) did Kent and Sussex finally cease to be part of Britain's front line. But, in the meantime, the people of Kent and Sussex would learn what it was like to be living on the site of a battlefield.

Chapter Seven

Life on the battlefield

Residents strolling in Alexandra Park... had a memorable thrill when eleven high explosive bombs fell there without exploding. Hastings and St Leonards in the Front Line, p. 14

As the Germans planned for invasion, and the defenders prepared their battlefield, the civilian population were trying to live something approximating to a normal life on it. It may first be worth recalling some of the regulations to which all citizens in wartime Britain were subject. Everyone was issued with a National Registration Identity Card and was required to show this on demand to any authorised person (but to nobody else). As a means of identification, they were relatively useless, since they had no photograph attached. People also had to carry their gas mask with them at all times (which they were supposed to wear for fifteen minutes per day, for acclimatisation purposes), along with their ration book, petrol coupons and the address of their next of kin, lest they should be killed as a result of enemy action.

Their car (if they had one) would have shrouded headlamps, no radio and would be immobilised, say by the removal of the rotor arm, if left unattended. (These regulations were elaborately detailed. Nobody under fourteen could officially 'attend' a car; one could not 'attend' more than one car at a time, and there were different standards of immobility applicable by day and night.) Once they got the car going again, journeys to anywhere unfamiliar became an adventure, as all signposts and other clues as to your whereabouts had been removed or obliterated. Even words such as 'Hastings Tramways Company' had to be removed from the sides of the council's vehicles. Asking for directions was no solution, since many people might well refuse to tell you, on the grounds that you may be a fifth columnist. Worse still, they might follow this advice from *Picture Post*:

> *With a view to misleading airborne invasion, I suggest the scheme of 'adopting' the name of one town by another town in a different locality. If, for example, all citizens in, say, Coventry, if met by a parachutist and asked the name of the town would at once reply 'This is Bristol', all residents in the same town would give the same reply.* Michael Glover. *Invasion Scare 1940*, Leo Cooper, 1999

Travelling on the wartime railways was equally fraught with difficulty, especially at night. Station name boards and other forms of identification were removed, and the blackout added to the difficulty of knowing where you were. Train windows were painted over and, at first, passengers travelled in stygian darkness, prompting this contribution from A A Milne in *Punch*:

> *We were alone, I hailed the fellow blindly, 'Excuse me, sir, I live at Wavertree. Is it the next but one?'* **She** *answered kindly, 'It was the last but three'.*

The Southern Railway locomotive St Lawrence, *after suffering a direct hit from a bomb on Cannon Street railway bridge, on 11 May 1941.*

Southern Railway, serving as it did the front-line areas of Britain, operated under the most difficult circumstances of any regional railway. It suffered around five times more incidents than any other company. Southern Railway alone suffered 58 air attacks on its trains between 1940 and 1943, and its total losses for the war were 190 locomotives lost or damaged, along with more than 4,000 carriages, 2,000 wagons and 199 bridges. Stations and railway lines were prime targets for bombers; Blenheim Road in Deal, which ran parallel to the railway and was near to the station, suffered particularly badly from bombing as a result. Trains visiting Dover became adept at hiding in the nearby tunnels during bombing raids and rolling stock was parked for safety in tunnels or on branch lines wherever they were available. Dover's Priory station suffered direct hits during an attack in September 1944; several people were killed and many more wounded. Even when trains were not directly hit, bomb damage to the lines could involve delay or rerouting for the passengers.

Special ambulance and evacuation trains were based at Tunbridge Wells during the early stages of the war, and later at Sevenoaks. Five emergency railheads were created for unloading them. These were by no means the only specialist rolling stock on the Southern Railway during the war years. Twelve armoured trains were built, two of which were deployed at Canterbury and Tonbridge. They consisted of a tank engine with armoured trucks, carrying a light anti-aircraft gun. These were kept constantly in steam until 1943, when invasion precautions were relaxed to some degree. Their functions were to patrol the line, to provide protection for railway staff carrying out repairs and, in the event of invasion, to provide a rallying point for Home Guards or regular troops. There were also super-heavy gun batteries mounted on railway wagons (some of which had their own dedicated trains). At the other extreme, as we saw, even the narrow-gauge Romney, Hythe and Dymchurch Railway was taken over by the military authorities.

When our traveller arrived home, there would be buckets of water and sand ready against the possibility of incendiary attack, the windows would be taped (against explosion) and (at night) securely blacked out. Reserves of food would walk the tightrope between a prudent reserve supply and hoarding. The telephone was for emergency use only and much of people's leisure time (after working long shifts, if they were in essential war industries) would be devoted to the Home Guard, ARP work or other war-related duties. As if all this were not enough, there were a host of minor wartime regulations to observe, covering everything from wasting food to kite-flying.

In May 1943, the viaduct carrying the Brighton-Lewes railway line was destroyed by a bomb. Remarkably, the service was restored within five weeks.

Labour shortages brought women into many traditionally male jobs. This one is jet-spraying oil and dirt from a locomotive.

Parliament passed the Emergency Powers (Defence) Act in 1939, which gave the Government draconian powers, requiring everybody 'to place themselves at the disposal of His Majesty.' But what exactly were people supposed to do? The usual suspects called for it to be used to introduce prohibition, or to prevent men consorting with women in swimsuits on the beaches. But eventually the management of the civilian role in the war fell to local Invasion Committees, established in each community. Among their duties was the preparation of War Books. These were to be drawn up in compliance with a standard format laid down by the Ministry of Home Security, and were to be destroyed 'should hasty evacuation become necessary.' Among other things, this required the Committee to identify: 'sites earmarked for mass graves, other means of conveying instructions and information to the public' (in the event of a total breakdown of normal communications in the community) and 'emergency transport, tools, plant, etc'.

Defence zones and evacuation areas

Further difficulties were put in the way of people entering the south-east coastal towns. From April 1940, the area became part of the snappily titled 'Medway, Thames and Dover area, consisting of the county of Kent and parts of Essex adjoining the Thames Estuary.' Introduced under the Emergency Powers (Defence) Act, this meant that alien citizens wanting to live in or even enter the area had to have the permission of the Chief Constable. He would need to know their name, nationality, occupation, the purpose of their visit and where they would stay. Those not granted permission to stay had to move out of a 20-mile zone around the coast of Kent and Sussex. They went in coaches, under police escort, many of them people long-established in their local business communities. Landladies soon started to be fined for not keeping records of any aliens lodging with them. By 20 June, an area 20 miles wide along the coastline between Rye and The Wash had been declared a Defence Zone. This meant that nobody could visit it without a permit. On 3 July, all beaches between Brighton and Selsey Bill were closed to the public.

Barbed-wire surrounds this seafront shelter at Sandgate, near Folkestone. Only the armed forces can bathe here.

The armed forces practise for gas raids. If it was supposed to be necessary for the children to wear gas masks, why do the soldiers not need them?

Rumours abounded: in May 1940, they forecast the imminent evacuation of Dover. The authorities acted firmly to dispel them:

> *The rumour which has been widely spread as to the evacuation of Dover is entirely without foundation. There is no intention to evacuate anyone, children or otherwise. Do NOT spread rumours.*

Do not believe the stories of threats to Dover. The advance of the Germans into Holland, however, makes more than ever necessary all the ARP precautions which have been dinned into the people's ears for months. Black out properly, back and front. Carry your gas mask. Keep under cover when there is gunfire. Put bonfires out before dusk.

The prospect of south-east Britain becoming a battleground, where the horrors of conventional warfare might be compounded by gas or chemical weapons, led the Government to review their policy on relocating children to areas like Kent and Sussex. Despite severe reservations on the part of Churchill and others, a parliamentary committee was even set up to investigate the possibility of evacuating the nation's children overseas. The scheme was deplored by many. The Chairman of Hastings Education Committee called it a 'fool scheme', pointing out that, at the planned rate of evacuation, it would take a hundred years to relocate them all overseas. Their authority alone had received 1,033 enquiries about the scheme and 593 completed application forms. He went on:

It is perfectly futile for parents to think they are going to get their children out of Hastings to the colonies in a few days and I think we ought to deprecate in the strongest possible way the movement of children from this area. Hastings and St Leonards Observer, 29 June 1940

It took the torpedoing of the ships *The City of Benares* and *Volendam* to bring an abrupt end to the overseas evacuation programme, but fuel was added to the fire of evacuation rumours when the Bishop of Chichester called in July 1940 for all parents who could do so to remove their children from the coastal areas. This led to a more general panic among the population, thinking that they should also move out. The local press ran a campaign calling upon everyone to 'stay put' pending any announcement from the Government. Rumours circulated in July 1940 that the Government was about to call for a voluntary evacuation of the coastal defence zone, prompting the Regional Commissioner to issue the following statement:

The Government is anxious that people should stay in their homes, and there is no change in the Government's view that the best assistance citizens can render to the defence of their country is to stay where they are and carry on their ordinary occupations. Hastings and St Leonards Observer, 13 July 1940

Despite this confirmation that the town not threatened, it was announced in the spring of 1940 that the Dover heavy artillery was going to practise between 8.00 am and sunset during June, July and August. The public would be given a week's notice, and would be expected to keep their windows open, to save them getting broken by the blast. The Germans claimed that Dover harbour had been bombed. It was not true, but newspaper reporters nonetheless flocked to the town to see the damage. Then, in July 1940, came the news that towns all along the south coast were to be declared Evacuation Areas for schoolchildren. This also included Margate, Ramsgate, Broadstairs, Sandwich, Deal and Folkestone (Hythe was added later):

> *Arrangements are being made for the despatch to safer districts in the Midlands and Wales of those children whose parents wish them to go. They will travel by special trains next Sunday.*

The move was voluntary, but local schools were to be closed and the teachers moved with them, in an effort to encourage children to go. Those children previously evacuated from London to within about 10 miles of the coasts of Suffolk, Essex, Kent and part of Norfolk were also being moved, this time compulsorily, to safer areas. A good number of local children (for example, about 3,000 Hastings children, or half of their school population) were kept behind and, as the *Dover Express* put it: 'without schools open for them, their future, educationally, is indeed parlous'. Pictures soon appeared in the local papers, showing the evacuated children enjoying the amenities of 'a Garden City in the Home Counties or somewhere in Hertfordshire'.

The ban on visiting most of the Sussex coast was eventually lifted in October 1942, at least temporarily, until the following March. People could still not take up permanent residence there and additional trips were by no means encouraged (there was no extra transport laid on, for example). But minutely detailed rules banning visits to specific administrative areas within Kent remained. How travellers were supposed to know when they were stepping from a permitted into a prohibited area, at a time when all signs giving a clue as to their location were banned, remains a mystery.

Cromwell!

Just before 7 September 1940, a variety of intelligence began to accumulate, suggesting that invasion could be imminent. Large numbers of vessels were assembling in the Channel ports and dive-bombers were gravitating towards the coastal airfields. German spies were picked up who said that their task was to report the movements of the British reserve forces to the north and west of London. The condition of the moon and tides also favoured a landing between 8 and 10 September.

Naval forces were put on immediate readiness, bombers designated to support the home forces were on half an hour's stand-by, but the army were still on eight hours' notice of possible invasion (this being the highest state of readiness they had, short of immediate action). It was decided that troops in the Southern and Eastern Commands would be brought to 'immediate action' and the signal 'Cromwell' was accordingly sent out to all units (this was the only practicable method for bringing the forces to this state of readiness – one short of actual invasion). This led to Home Guard commanders in different parts of the country calling out their forces under the mistaken belief that the invasion was actually in progress. Church bells were rung, reinforcing the belief among the general public that the skies were already thick with German paratroops, and a welter of rumours began to circulate. The Germans obligingly added to the atmosphere of hysteria with an air raid on London and nervous officers blew up some of the mined bridges, for example at Brooks Gate, Boons Hill and Knock, near Rye.

The following day, General Brooke had to make it clear that church bells should be rung only if the member of the Home Guard concerned had personally seen more than twenty-five paratroops descending, and that the signal 'Cromwell' was not a general call-out for the Home Guard, but only applied to specialised units.

> # Despite Hitler's Hates
> ## and
> ## Nazi Nastiness
> ### THE
> # Burlington Bars
> ## WOOLCOMBER STREET,
> ## are still undamaged
> ## and carrying on.

Such was the uncertainty of the business climate that this establishment found it necessary to advertise that it was still open.

Everybody's talking

> *Dame rumour... has been busy in Tunbridge Wells spreading all sorts of ridiculous rumours in which even some of our prominent and respected tradesmen are implicated. One of the victims is Mr James Toop, the well-known butcher, whose absence from business for a few days was seized upon as sufficient evidence that he had been interned. The simple fact is Mr Toop is engaged on Government service in connection with national meat distribution. It would be much better if busybodies occupied themselves in work of national importance, rather than spreading stupid stories about those who are doing their bit to help their country in its hour of need.* Kent and Sussex Courier, 24 May 1940

The fruitless search for the non-existent fifth column was pursued with great enthusiasm. No sign, however improbable, was ignored. Vigilant eyes fell upon the following code, chalked on a Hastings wall in June 1940:

YYURYYUBICURYY4M

Had the public known about them, there would doubtless have been calls for this to be fed into the Enigma decoding machines at Bletchley Park, until someone pointed out that it was in fact a schoolboy riddle (translation: 'Too wise you are, too wise you be, I see you are too wise for me'). The editor solemnly warned against similar pranks, on the grounds that they would help mask the activities of the real fifth column. Being named as a fifth columnist could be traumatic for the individual concerned. A Tunbridge Wells rag-and-bone man who was singled out for this treatment ended up drowning himself in a pond, thinking he was about to be arrested.

German radio did their bit for the rumour mill, reporting that their paratroopers had been dropped near Dover, and that the authorities were keeping it quiet. A similar rumour was spread by Tunbridge Wells telephone operator Walter Page, claiming that twenty German paratroopers had landed near Hawkhurst. But, unlike Goebbels, he was not immune from prosecution and was fined £25 by the authorities. The editor of the *Dover Express* railed against the media coverage his town was getting:

> *The greatest indignation is felt in Dover about the sensational stories being sent to the London newspapers and elsewhere about Dover. The published efforts of these correspondents, added to lying rumours, were doing definite work for the Fifth Column.*
>
> *All this press scare publicity has undoubtedly had the effect of inducing many to leave Dover. Obviously, those with no real ties with civil defence or who are not engaged in the industries that are essential for Dover and public services are quite well advised to take an early summer holiday. On the other hand, work must and will proceed. Those thrown out of employment in one industry should make a determined effort to enrol at the earliest moment in one of those doing work of national importance elsewhere.* Dover Express and East Kent News, 31 May 1940

Nobody's talking!

If people in Dover were unhappy with the press coverage they were getting, some in Hastings later that year were unhappy about the coverage their town was not

If being shelled by heavy guns was not exciting enough for you, you could always arrange to be fired from one.

ROYAL HIPPODROME

WANTED !!

THE BRAVEST GIRL IN DOVER !

To be fired from

THE GREAT LEVANTE'S Electric Cannon

at the Second House — Tuesday Night.

HEIGHT: 5 ft.   **WEIGHT: 8 st.**

Apply:—THE MANAGER, HIPPODROME, DOVER.

Between 9 a.m. and 12 noon, or after 5 p.m.

ALEXANDER BOTTLE & Co.,
CHEMISTS,
37, TOWNWALL STREET, DOVER.
September, 1940.

NOTICE TO CUSTOMERS

We very much regret to inform you that owing to enemy action, our premises and stock have been extensively damaged.

In the circumstances we find it impossible to carry on, and we are therefore temporarily closing the business. We hope to re-open again as soon as we are able to do so.

May we take this opportunity of thanking you for your past favours, and express the hope that we may continue to serve you once again in the years of peace that are to come. 10825 J27

As if depopulation and the loss of tourism were not enough for businesses in the coastal towns, many were forced to close as a direct result of air raids or shelling.

getting. They were being bombed, and nobody was talking about it!

Is it not time Hastings had a little of the publicity which London gets from the press? It is all London. 'London can take it', 'London keeps its chin up'. Well, I am sure Hastings (and St Leonards) does so, and as to 'Cockney Grit' there is plenty of Sussex ditto, but it is not blazoned abroad.

I am not trying to decry or belittle the courage of the Londoners, but lives lost and homes destroyed here are just as hard luck for the victims here and yet one does not hear our town bewail its fate. Letter to the *Hastings and St Leonards Observer*, 19 October 1940

Not only was nobody talking about it, but nobody appeared to be doing anything about it. It was a town of no strategic importance which just happened to receive a good many bombs, so they sent a petition to the king to ask for their own anti-aircraft defences. But a resident of St Leonards started what can best be described as a spirited correspondence in the local newspaper when he advanced the view that Britain's limited anti-aircraft defences could be better used elsewhere. 'If this town and every person in it were wiped out, would it help the Germans to conquer the British Empire?' he asked. As the Luftwaffe began planning its invasion preparations in earnest, Kent and Sussex began to get its share of bombing. One early attack struck 'an East Sussex village', as the local press rather imprecisely described it under the censorship guidelines (the Ministry of

The danger from air raids did not end with the sounding of the all-clear.

A WARNING TO EVERYONE

Apparently in their week-end raids on this country the Germans dropped a considerable number of delayed action bombs, and as they may be buried people should avoid approaching any suspicious-looking craters. Many of these bombs have been known to explode several hours afterwards, and therefore caution should be carried to the extreme.

The Biggest Bang

Almost certainly the loudest explosion to be heard on the battlefield awoke the population of Newhaven (and others many miles away) at about 5.00 am on 22 November 1944. A British barge carrying about 180 tons of high explosive broke loose from its tow and struck a mine. The blast damaged almost every building in town, blew out windows in Lewes, seven miles away, was felt in Hailsham twelve miles away and heard even further afield. Miraculously, due to the early hour, there were no fatalities and few casualties resulting from the explosion.

Home Security was even more vague, referring to it only as one of 'two districts in south-east England'). The paper reported with evident satisfaction that the total casualties were one pony and forty chickens. Damage was limited to a chicken run, an empty stable and some chicken coops, but a local resident said 'We feel like the western front now.'

From 12 August 1940, Dover and surrounding towns had shelling from the German coastal guns to add to their miseries. The nickname for their area was changed from 'Hellfire Corner' to 'Shellfire Corner'. The source of the explosions was at first a mystery – no aircraft had been heard – but the calibre of the shells, worked out from their shrapnel, indicated that they were from long-range artillery. Local people soon got to know that there was a gap of seventy-two seconds between the flash of a heavy gun on the French coast and the arrival of its shell, and became adept at running for the nearest shelter in that period.

Those in peril on the sea...

Fishermen continued their hazardous occupations, despite the hostilities. One benefit of the war was that all limits on the size of net meshes were suspended. The Sussex Sea Fisheries Committee ruled that 'all fish is food and we want all we can get.' Good catches were reported, despite fishing being limited to the daylight hours. There was also the unexpected bonus of hordes of stunned fish to be found floating on the surface of the sea after the air raids on Dover and the other ports. But this was small compensation when the normal dangers of the fisherman's job were compounded by the possibility of enemy attack – the Rye trawler *Mitzpah* lost two of its crew to German strafing. Nor were they helped by the activities of their own side. The bodies of the crew of the Hastings trawler *Happy Return* were washed ashore, some weeks after their boat failed to return to port. The boat was finally located and a diver concluded that they had trawled up a mine. A similar fate was thought to have befallen a fisherman at Lydd. The problem stemmed from the navy's practice of sinking, rather than detonating, German mines. A fisherman explained:

> *These mines are fired at by rifles and sunk by penetrating the air chamber. Unless the mines are blown up they will be a constant source of danger to fishermen after the war.* Dover Express and East Kent News, 5 January 1940

Questions were asked about the matter in Parliament, and members were told that it was not practicable to blow up all enemy mines. Most mines sunk by rifle fire were rendered harmless, but destructor ships were to be introduced to pull up the mines and make them safe – if the trawlers did not find them first.

But fishermen were not the only ones to face hazards from stray mines:

> *Residents of a nearby coast town were awakened shortly after 2am on Monday by a terrific explosion which shook the town. The cause of the explosion was the blowing up of a mine which, washed ashore, struck part of a new promenade. The promenade, which is at the foot of the cliffs and on the sands within the harbour, has been constructed within the last two years.* Dover Express and East Kent News, 2 February 1940

This was one of several mines washed ashore that week. Windows were broken and furniture thrown about the rooms of houses by the explosion. But even a mine could be profitable for an enterprising and observant person. The Admiralty, presumably deciding that patriotism was not incentive enough, started a reward scheme. It paid up to £1,000 for information leading to the capture or destruction of an enemy warship, £50 for information about the whereabouts of such vessels, down to £5 for information about mines, parachute mines or 'other objects of enemy origin'.

Looking was one thing – touching quite another. When items from a recently sunken steamer were washed up on Hastings beach in April 1940, the authorities issued a stern warning to people not to remove them. They were the property of the Minister of Shipping, and anyone spotting them should report it to their local Receiver of Wrecks.

By late 1940, some three or four hundred residents of 'a south-east coastal town' (Hastings) were sheltering nightly in caves in the cliffs. The local authority laid on electricity, hot and cold running water and a coal-fired kitchen range. Some of the residents were permanent, having been bombed out, and had brought what remained of their furniture with them. Separate areas were set aside for recreation and communal meals were served in a nearby centre. It was, someone observed, 'a cosy and most respectable "underworld"' in St Martin's Caves.

The Town Council saw it as their duty to lay down rules for the conduct of people in shelters. There was much debate as to whether singing should be allowed. Their rules said 'No smoking, singing or playing of a musical instrument, except with the permission of the local authority or in places set apart for that purpose,' but supporters of singing argued that it was a valuable way of keeping up the spirits. One eventuality for which they may not have legislated occurred when Elsie Ball and William Coussens had their wedding ceremony at St Johns, Upper St Leonards, interrupted by an air raid. The entire congregation adjourned to the shelter, where the organist requisitioned a piano provided there (hopefully with the council's permission) and the nuptials were completed just as the all-clear sounded.

It was not just unlawful singing that went on in the shelters. The Emergency Committee of Tunbridge Wells Borough Council learned that the Albion Road shelter was being used for unspecified 'immoral purposes'. Other shelters were being occupied by people of no fixed abode and had become verminous as a result.

Dover residents were one of several communities to retreat to caves to shelter from the German bombs.

One of the unofficial residents even died there. A number of the shelters suffered vandalism. The Town Clerk was instructed to draw up model rules and regulations for the use of shelters and many had to be kept locked, except during alerts.

Ghost towns and financial ruin

The partial evacuation of the coastal towns marked the beginning of a calamitous spiral of decline in their wartime fortunes. As the children left, so schools were closed down and non-teaching staff were laid off. Those of alien extraction had already been moved out. The loss of cross-Channel and holiday trade put large numbers out of work and invasion fears led many of those who could do so to move away from the area. Others signed up for the armed forces and went to serve their country. There were other, involuntary, evacuations; Captain Robert Cecil Gordon-Canning, a member of The Link, a pro-Nazi organisation, was forced to leave his home in Sandwich, within a Defence Area, and was subsequently arrested under the Defence Regulations, as were many pre-war Fascist-sympathisers.

The populations of the coastal towns plummeted. Margate's peacetime population of around 40,000 had fallen by August 1940 to just 11,516. This in turn finished off many local businesses which depended upon the town's population for their trade. Publicans began applying to the licensing magistrates to close their establishments down for the duration and even the churches started closing. Wartime Saturday afternoons in their High Streets started to look like peacetime Sunday mornings (before Sunday shop opening). National chains of estate agents started advertising in the local papers, offering leases on business premises in towns elsewhere in the country, unaffected by the Defence Area and other regulations besetting the south-east coast. But perhaps the most total depopulation occurred on the Downs between Brighton and Eastbourne, where the entire village of Stanmer, home to a hundred people, with twenty cottages, village shop and parish church, was abandoned to allow the army to use the area for exercises. There was also the dramatic disappearance of Bungalow Town at Shoreham, evacuated at forty-eight hours' notice by Montgomery and subsequently demolished, so as not to interfere with the field of fire for his guns.

The carefree pre-war tourist days were by now a distant memory, though the occasional hardy visitor still braved the seafront. One was hardier than most: Guy Gibson, soon to be leader of the Dambusters and a VC, was in the area to witness a test of Barnes Wallis's bouncing bomb:

> We had been told that things weren't quite ready, so we drove round to the town of Margate to see what it looked like in time of war. It was pretty hard to realise, as we lounged on the beach, that this was the same old sunshine resort of peacetime; the hotels were all closed; Dreamland was an army barracks; barbed-wire was everywhere, and the place was full of soldiers. The only thing that had remained was the fish. We had just stuffed ourselves full of Dover soles and now felt pleasantly lazy in the afternoon, listening to the screaming of the gulls as they glided over the harbour. Suddenly there was a noise like the release of compressed air, then the chattering of cannon guns, followed by the full crump of bombs. Like a flash, glinting in the sun at 'nought' feet, four FW 190s rocketed over our heads going flat out for France, followed closely by four Typhoons. The many Bofors parked along the front chattered after them, sending up red balls one after another in a gentle curve towards the whole ensemble, enemy and friend. Rootes, p. 137

The war was a financial disaster for the local authorities concerned, who saw their rates income plummet as people moved out. Dover Council by June 1940 found itself with an overdraft of £30,000 and Margate had to introduce a radical rate-relief scheme for those who relied upon income from visitors, and had seen their incomes disappear. The needy were only required to pay 30 per cent of their normal rates bills. Margate's income from the rates between April and October fell from £220,000 in 1939 to just £61,500 in 1940, and their arrears rocketed from £10,000 to £33,800. At around the same time, Dover issued a warning that those leaving properties should keep on paying their rates, unless they promised never to return to the vacant property. For his part, the Chairman of Hastings' Finance Committee was at pains to point out that the town was not technically bankrupt, although the most rigid economy would have to be practised. Local dignitaries

Some front-line towns – a league table of damage from German bombing

Town	Numbers of houses destroyed
Dover (including rural district)	946
Canterbury	808
Eastbourne	475
Hastings and St Leonards	463
Ramsgate	393
Chatham	297
Dartford (including rural district)	294
Folkestone	290
Rochester	276
Margate	268
Brighton	200 (approx)
Ashford	184
Gillingham	168
Sevenoaks (including rural district)	128
Maidstone	127
Battle	105
Hythe	96
Swanscombe	93
Whitstable	84
Bexhill	81

Sources: Rootes, p. 200: *Sussex Express and County Herald* (various). Figures for Dover and some other Kent towns will include damage from coastal artillery.

began lobbying Government, saying that the burden should be shared nationally, rather than being borne entirely by local people.

Questions were asked in Parliament about the plight of the coastal authorities and the Government eventually agreed to help them out, in those cases where the machinery of Local Government was felt to be in danger of breaking down. But at first this was only in the form of interest-free loans that had to be repaid, rather than grants. Under further pressure, they eventually relented and agreed that only 25 per cent of the debt need be repaid after the war. Despite all their problems, the councils were still berated for their spending on non-essential items. 'Bumbledom' was the name popularly coined for it. Why, thundered the *Dover Express*, was the council still building an infants' school and installing water mains, when all their efforts should be devoted to national defence?

More rules and regulations

The Regional Commissioner introduced a 10.00 pm curfew for theatres and cinemas in the Defence Area in September 1940. The Borough Engineer of Hastings had already trumped this by introducing a 9.00 pm curfew for public conveniences within days of hostilities starting. To add to the feeling of desolation, Hastings and some other coastal towns also imposed a night-time curfew on their seafronts.

Courting couples who lost track of the time in seafront shelters or people simply trying to find their way home through darkened streets would find themselves arrested and hauled up before the courts. In some other towns, the front was open all hours as usual, give or take the barbed-wire and mines. None of this deterred a Folkestone man, who persisted in breaking his way through the beach defences, in order to pursue his hobby of sea-bathing. He was eventually imprisoned for three months, being described by the judge as a danger to himself and others.

The mixed experiences of child evacuees have been well documented, but less has been written about the elderly people who were evacuated from coastal areas like Kent and Sussex. In July 1940 the *Dover Express* carried the story of a couple who had been evacuated to a place called Ilex Lodge, in the West Country. This was an institution which evidently still operated a particularly ferocious version of the Victorian Poor Law. Right up to the Second World War, this legislation – dating essentially from 1834 – provided much of what passed for Britain's social services. According to the couple, they were put into single-sex accommodation and were not even allowed to speak to their spouses, except for two hours a week during church services. Strict silence was observed during mealtimes (the meals consisting to a large degree of bread and margarine, and tea) and they even tried to get the women evacuees to wear the uniforms of poorhouse inmates. The hours of rising (7.00 am) and retiring (8.00 pm) were also strictly regulated. The authorities were at pains to deny any stories of ill-treatment.

Kent and Sussex had its share of conscientious objectors, and employers agonised about what to do with them – in particular, the local authorities, who agonised in public. There was general agreement that they should not gain advantage in the promotion or any other employment stakes while their former

Local authorities were forced to pursue those fleeing the area to recover their rent and rates.

PUBLIC NOTICES.

BOROUGH   OF DOVER.

NOTICE as to LIABILITY for RENTS and RATES

In order to avoid any possible misunderstanding, occupiers of houses who have left, or who intend to leave, the town are hereby notified that they remain liable to their landlords for rent until the expiry of the period of notice required under their agreement and the complete vacation of their houses by the removal of all furniture. They are also liable for rates and should notify the date of their removal to the Rates Dept., Maison Dieu House.

S. R. H. LOXTON,
Town Clerk.

Brook House, Dover.
5th June, 1940.

The people of Maidstone pick their way through the bomb damage, following an air raid in October 1940.

Time is food —

PLOUGH NOW!

— between the stooks if possible

Apart from present arable, two million more acres of grassland must be ploughed to meet the nation's needs. Start NOW, or demands on available machinery will be too great next Spring. Early ploughing means early sowing and early sowing means better crops.

"The cultivation that should be done in the next few months will have a very definite effect on the yield of the harvest next year ... Time is definitely food. We must see that not a moment is lost."
— The Minister of Agriculture speaking in the House of Commons on July 24, 1941.

ISSUED BY THE MINISTRY OF AGRICULTURE AND FISHERIES

The lack of imported food created pressure to maximise home production – nowhere (apart from a few bowling greens) was exempt.

colleagues were away performing their national duty. After Maidstone Town Council decided that they would only retain conscientious objectors in their employ on the same terms and conditions as their equivalents in the forces, Dover Council went one better and decided not to employ them at all, and Hastings voted to sack the two they had on their books. Kent County Council decided to do the same and set up an inquiry to winkle out any such people among their staff – a body likened by one councillor to a cross between Star Chamber and the Holy Inquisition.

They were not the only workers to get into trouble with their employers. In January 1942 the miners at Betteshanger Colliery struck over pay. This was illegal under wartime regulations and the nineteen-day strike was broken by some fifty of them being taken to court. Most were fined, but the ringleaders were sentenced to hard labour. Those who were jailed were treated as heroes within their communities on their release and were reinstated by their employers. Most of those fined refused to pay their fines – the prisons were too full to take them.

Even the most innocent-sounding activities became off-limits. A Folkestone schoolteacher was fined 10 shillings for photographing a bombed house, and a photographer working under contract for a national newspaper (newspaper and photographer each thought the other had the requisite permit) was fined £10 for the same offence. A Hastings man was even fined £2 for photographing an electricity pylon. Yet at the same time, the *Hastings Observer* was publishing pictures of bomb damage in its pages and even offering to supply copies to its readers for a small charge.

A Dutchman got six months in prison for visiting Canterbury without the appropriate permit. He thought that the letter he bore from the commanding officer of Eastern Command gave him the authority to do so. Travel within 5 miles of the coast was prohibited without a permit. Even a motor-cyclist, driving into Dover to collect his permit, found himself arrested and brought before the courts. This piece of over-zealous enforcement was dismissed by the courts, but plenty of others found themselves fined. The public were also reminded that, as few people knew, the use of torches or even smoking in the street was prohibited during air raids, lest the glow of a cigarette-end gave useful signals to the enemy, flying 5 miles above.

The changing fortunes of war could affect even something as fundamental as your nationality. Philip di Marco, son of a Sussex confectioner, decided in early June 1940 to renounce his British citizenship and revert to his Italian origins.

So intensive was the drive for home-grown food that even roadside grass verges were used in some areas.

Among other considerations, this enabled him to avoid being drafted into the British armed forces. Within days, Mussolini declared war and he was arrested as an enemy alien.

People began to learn the meaning of total war. First, it was announced that all the flowerbeds in the parks of Hastings were to be given over to the cultivation of vegetables. Where the pansies once bloomed in Warrior Square Gardens, onions would be grown for use in the communal feeding centres. Beds of watercress filled the stream at the Bohemia Nursery. The local press even managed to wax lyrical about the ornamental properties of vegetables. Golf courses and playing fields were to be let to a farmer for grazing in the effort to become more self-sufficient in food. Prior to this, it had been decreed that, to save petrol, all playing fields in West Sussex would have to be mowed by hand. Only the bowling greens were spared the indignity of being turned over to sheep. Then, as Christmas 1940 approached, the first female 'postmen' since 1918 were seen on the streets. They were followed the next year by women bus conductors.

The need to save raw materials led to some places of entertainment weighing, rather than counting, their takings. The Opera House at Tunbridge Wells offered a free cinema show for any child turning up with at least 2lb of waste paper for recycling. The lure of a combination of cartoons and Ministry of Information propaganda features proved (in varying proportions) irresistible and the management ended up with a packed house and more than 4 tons of waste paper to deal with.

The shops in Hastings found a new way of competing. An advertising feature in September 1940 promoted the merits of their respective air-raid shelters. Compton's boasted that 'magazines are provided for the use and comfort of customers during air raid warnings,' while Wilshin's more practically offered candles, sal volatile and first-aid equipment. But for the safety-conscious diner, it had to be the Kings Café: 'All meals are served in our light, airy air raid shelter, which is entirely below ground level.' Not all retailers were so accommodating. Shops in Tunbridge Wells were criticised by the local paper for turfing their customers out to fend for themselves as soon as an air-raid warning sounded. This was felt to discourage country folk from coming into the town to shop:

If we are to share in a real sense with the glorious achievements of our airmen we must not waste a minute of working energy. Ways and means should be found of carrying on business while a raid is in progress. Kent and Sussex Courier, 20 September 1940

The *Hastings Observer's* restaurant correspondent seemed to have left his critical faculties at home when he visited the new Communal Feeding Centre in West Street. 'For 8d I had a first-rate meal. There was steaming hot cottage pie and vegetables, with an ample helping of suet pudding and jam to follow. The food was excellent, the service splendid and the kitchen was spotlessly clean.' And not a word about the wine list.

Thus was everyday life conducted on the battlefield. But what would life have been like if the Germans had come?

Chapter Eight

What if...?

Hitler and his close entourage received the news of their victory with as much relief as joy. The latest of his gambles had come off. Kenneth Macksey. *Invasion: The Invasion of England July 1940*, Collier Macmillan, 1980 – one of the counter-factual histories speculating on the outcome of an attempted invasion – p. 205

What would have happened, had Hitler gone ahead with the invasion plan? This is one of the great unanswered questions of modern history. It offers limitless scope for speculation, not least since the 'what ifs' can be taken back and back through the conduct of the war:

- What if Goering had persisted with the bombing of RAF airfields, rather than switching his attention to London?
- What if the Luftwaffe had gone for RAF airfields from the start, rather than attacking the convoys?
- What if the Luftwaffe had appreciated the importance of British radar and its associated command and communications structures, and had concentrated their attacks on them accordingly?
- What if the Germans had attempted the invasion immediately after Dunkirk, when Britain was at its most exposed?
- What if Guderian had not halted his panzers' advance just outside Dunkirk, and had prevented the Dunkirk evacuation?
- What if Gort and the British Expeditionary Force had turned south, to join the rest of the Allied armies as the Germans advanced, rather than north towards Dunkirk?
- What if Hitler had launched Operation *Yellow*, the invasion of the Low Countries, in November 1939 as originally planned, giving more time to plan and execute *Sea Lion* before the winter weather intervened in 1940?
- What if he had conceived the invasion of the Low Countries as a launch-pad for the invasion of Britain, and had begun the planning for it at the same time?
- What if Halifax, rather than Churchill, had succeeded Chamberlain as Prime Minister?

And so the list goes on. Because there are so many variables, once one starts rearranging history in this way it becomes possible to argue the case for almost any outcome. Not only that, but the *ex post facto* strategists have not only the wisdom of hindsight but also infinitely better intelligence than was available to either side at the time, to help them become better military strategists than Hitler or Goering (never a particularly high hurdle, in any event). So rather than hypothesise a particular series of events, leading to a particular outcome, we will look instead at some of the factors on which the success or failure of any invasion would have hinged.

Timing: this would have been essential to the outcome of the exercise and it is notable that two of the counter-factual historians who have written speculative 'accounts' of a successful invasion (Macksey (1980) and Stephen Badsey in *Tsouras* (ed) (2002)) moved the German landing to July, when the British home defences were at their least-prepared and the weather was likely to be at its kindest. The two-month delay between then and Hitler's planned September invasion date gave the British the opportunity to add almost a thousand fighters to its strength, to complete its chain of radar stations and to add significantly to its anti-aircraft and other defences, as well as starting to rebuild the army that had been shattered at Dunkirk. Such a timetable would, however, have required the Germans to have started serious planning for invasion much sooner than they did and, for this to happen, Hitler would have had to take a very different view about the likelihood of a negotiated settlement with Britain.

Control of the air: this was one vital pre-requisite on which all parts of the German armed forces were agreed. Without it, the invasion forces were not safe in their ports of embarkation, at any point in the Channel crossing or during the landing. There were two elements to gaining this control (although the Germans did not appreciate the significance of the second of them) – the destruction of Fighter Command and its airfields, and the neutralising of British radar and its associated command and communications structure. As long as the British radar and its communications remained relatively intact, the effectiveness of Fighter Command was enormously enhanced. Without it, the field of vision of the British pilots would have been reduced from about 120 miles to little more than what they could see from their cockpits. Perseverance in attacking the stations would have paid dividends greater than almost anything the Luftwaffe might have achieved against the fighters and their airfields.

The factors that told against the Luftwaffe gaining aerial superiority are discussed elsewhere in the book. The lack of range of the Bf109 fighter was critical. While they were limited to flying from airfields in northern France, they could not escort bombers beyond the north-west tip of London. Raids on airfields beyond that became a hazardous proposition, and fighters from airfields to the north and west of London could still have taken on German forces attacking London or even targets further south (though their ability to make a timely interception may have become problematic, and the range of the Spitfires themselves may well itself have become an issue). Destruction of the south-eastern airfields would also have limited the role Fighter Command could have played in attacking invading forces in the Channel or in northern France.

Control of the Channel: the Royal Navy had a vast numerical superiority over their German opposition, but the effectiveness of this would have depended upon a number of factors:

- How total would German control of the airspace above the Channel be? Early reverses for the Royal Navy (and events throughout the war) were to reveal how vulnerable capital ships were to aerial attack. The dangers here would have been compounded by the existence of the coastal batteries and the lack of space for manoeuvre in the narrow waters of the Strait;

• How effectively in the longer term could the Germans have defended their Channel-crossing corridor? In addition to air cover, the corridor would need to have been protected with a combination of mines, U-boats, coastal guns and such surface vessels as they could mobilise. This would need to be effective, not just for the initial attack, but over a period of weeks and months, as they reinforced and supplied their invading troops. Even if the Home Fleet failed, the Germans were likely to have faced successive onslaughts from various Royal Navy fleets, stationed around the world and recalled home as the threat to the home country became ever more urgent;

• One factor over which the Germans would have had no control was the forces of nature. Moonlight and tides set quite narrow windows of opportunity for landing, and they would have to have taken whatever these opportunities presented, in terms of weather, currents and other navigational problems. The *Sea Lion* fleet was vast, unwieldy and, in many cases, of questionable seaworthiness. One German admiral described the motley fleet

Churchill tanks being taken to exercises by train. Not only did it save valuable petrol, but it was probably quicker than them going under their own power.

as 'Formation Pigpile'. They would have been travelling by night, in close formation (to maximise air cover) and would probably have been under attack for much or all of the journey, from embarkation to landing. So the likelihood of them ramming each other, being sunk, or trying to land at the wrong place at the wrong time looked considerable, and would increase significantly with adverse weather.

Logistics: as we have seen, the German army's ideal was to land a very large number of soldiers in a very short period of time, across a very wide front. The navy wanted exactly the opposite of this. The realities of control of the Channel meant that the initial landing would have to have been on a very much smaller scale, the build-up much more gradual and the front much narrower than the army wanted. But the more successful the navy were at getting people ashore, the bigger the problem of keeping them supplied became. The same transport that was needed to carry successive waves of men and their weapons to Britain would also be needed to keep the entire force supplied. Each division needed an absolute minimum of 300 tons a day, according to Fleming. So even the first eleven divisions of the *Sea Lion* force required 3,300 tons of supplies shipping across the Channel daily, once they were fully landed. A narrow beach-head also reduced the options for finding new places to land supplies, without the invasion forces making considerable progress overland.

The fleet that was relied upon to make these deliveries was a finite resource (there were no reserves of ships, and no immediate prospects of making good losses). Moreover, it was a resource that had been borrowed, at great cost to the rest of the German economy. Every week it was away from its normal duties harmed their economy and undermined the ability of the Germans to conduct the war in the longer term. (Had it been away from Germany much beyond the middle of September, for example, it would apparently have delayed the delivery of fertilisers to German agriculture, with adverse effects for the 1941 harvest). It was also a potentially diminishing resource, much of it being unsuited to sea-borne travel, and was subject each trip to the same dangers that would have faced it on the initial journey. The shipping resources available for resupplying the invading forces and landing reinforcements were thus likely to reduce significantly, just as the demands upon them increased.

Fleming sees this as one of the Achilles' heels of the entire project. He estimates that, even with Folkestone and Dover captured and back in working order (the delays to which would depend upon how thoroughly the British wrecked them before abandoning them) the two ports could only have supplied two-fifths of even the initial forces' daily needs. This is without them being needed to play any part in the landing of further reinforcements, or supplying their separate needs. The alternative, of landing onto open beaches, was dangerous, insecure and extremely inefficient, which was why the Allies went to the huge lengths of building the Mulberry harbours for D-Day.

However, Fleming seems to ignore the part that aerial supply might have played. According to Macksey, the Luftwaffe at that time had the capability of delivering 3,000 tons of supplies in a single drop, and were capable of making two deliveries a day from bases in northern France. They had largely supplied the earlier invasion of Norway. But this again begs a number of questions, such as:

- Would the entire transport fleet of the Luftwaffe have been available to this battlefront?
- How would the competing demands of delivering more troops and their additional equipment have been balanced against those of supplying the existing troops?
- How would the demands for space for transport planes on British airfields have weighed against the pressing need to get fighters into advanced positions at the earliest opportunity?
- What airfields were they to use, given that their prior objective had been to bomb all the airfields between London and the invasion coast into an unusable state, immediately prior to the invasion, and given that they might not have access to the facilities for restoring them that were open to the British? (One of Churchill's complaints was that the Royal Air Force relied too much upon civilian contractors for this work.)
- How well equipped were they to transport the supplies from wherever they were landed in Britain (be it beach, port or airfield) to the troops on what they hoped would be an ever-expanding front?

The final factor in this equation was the scope for the invading forces to live off the land. As we have seen, this was given as a specific objective for the troops, since the German authorities recognised the difficulty of resupplying them in the short term. In the more urbanised areas, this might have been a possibility, depending upon how far the local population took on board their Government's instructions to deny the invaders access to all resources. In the rural areas like the Romney Marshes, remote and deliberately depopulated, the prospects looked very limited indeed.

This seems to be *par excellence* a piece of alternative history where you make your assumptions and you draw your conclusions accordingly. Overall, the initial invasion seems a hugely risky project. In the event of imminent attack, the invasion ports could have expected to be bombed by the RAF and shelled by the Royal Navy. Neutralising Fighter Command in the south-east prior to invasion would not necessarily have silenced Bomber Command, although it would have enormously increased the dangers for them of attacking the French coast. Bombing and shelling would have made the orderly embarkation of large numbers of troops and horses an extremely difficult process (though not impossible, as Dunkirk proved). This would have been just a prelude to the effects of a journey of possibly thirteen hours, where seasickness in the poorly ventilated barges would have been compounded by aerial, naval and eventually coastal bombardment, possibly followed also by gas attacks and all the other opposition on the beaches.

However, if the Germans had managed to get a significant force ashore, there does not seem to have been a great deal to impede their progress, certainly in the early days after Dunkirk. This was the main time when a determined attack, even by a relatively small force, might have succeeded. As Fleming put it:

At this time... there simply did not exist in the islands the physical means of repelling, or even containing, a determined attack. The BEF, dead tired, disorganised, without artillery or transport, had temporarily ceased to cohere as a force; units, much depleted, could have been sent into action, but formations existed as such only on paper. A few half-trained and much less than half-equipped divisions, which had not been fit to send to France, could have been moved – by rail – to meet the incursion, whose progress would not have been seriously hindered by the Local Defence Volunteers, most of whom were still in the Brassard and shotgun stage. Fleming, pp. 298-9

Those in command of the British forces put it no less bluntly. Brooke commented as follows (and this was him writing in September, almost four months after Dunkirk):

Our exposed coastline is just twice the length of the front line the French were holding in France with about eighty divisions and a Maginot Line! Here we have about 22 divisions of which only half can be looked upon as in any way fit for any form of mobile operation! Danchev and Todman, 15 September 1940

Kieser describes Churchill and General Thorne, Commander of the XII Corps (guarding Kent), discussing the matter over lunch at Chequers on 30 June 1940. Thorne forecast the landing of some 80,000 men between Thanet and Pevensey, and could see them probing the Allied defences to find a weak point. Thorne himself could see no way of preventing the Germans from driving through Canterbury, directly towards London. In similar vein, the Chiefs of Staff acknowledged:

Should the Germans succeed in establishing a force with its vehicles in this country, our army forces have not got the offensive power to drive it out. Collier, p. 124)

We may have good reason to be grateful that this was one part of Battlefield Britain where the battle did not materialise.

What if? The civilian experience of invasion

Another aspect of the speculation about invasion concerns the fate of the civilian population in that event. Would they have followed Churchill's injunction and fought the invaders to the last man (and possibly woman and child)? Or would there have been the same mixture of covert resistance, sullen acquiescence and active collaboration as was seen in occupied Europe? Parker argues that the will to resist was far greater in Britain than in France, where the Third Republic was unpopular and the nation divided. Some French writers, he says, welcomed German control, rather than the incompetent government of their fellow countrymen; while others in France welcomed Fascism as a bulwark against Communism and some were prepared to accept almost any form of government as being less bad than war. In Britain, support for King, Country and the Government was much more united. Churchill's support in wartime opinion polls scarcely ever fell below 80 per cent. On the other hand, there was also evidence of widespread low morale. Ponting quotes Lord Clark's experience on an Emergency Committee on Home Morale:

> *The only interesting feature was the amount of evidence that came in on how low morale in England was, much lower than anyone had ever dared to say. But there was obviously nothing we could do about it.* 28 May 1940: Clive Ponting. *1940: Myth and Reality,* Hamish Hamilton, 1990

Apart from the training given to the Home Guard, the civilian population appears to have been given relatively little guidance about what to do in the event of invasion. The key instruction in 1940 was to stay put, in order to avoid the kind of chaos caused on the continent by floods of refugees clogging the roads. The large-scale nightly exoduses from major cities affected by German bombing suggest that this instruction might have been quite widely disregarded. Even the advice leaflet 'Beating the Invader' issued by the Ministry of Information in May 1941 was very limited in its scope. It can be summarised as 'Carry on as normal for as long as possible; only take orders from uniformed British officials; don't hoard food; listen to the wireless for instructions or look on official Ministry of Information notice boards; immobilise your car and hide your bicycle and your maps.'

Some local newspapers carried more detailed instructions about the roles of civilians in the event of invasion, including some quaintly sexist divisions of labour. They had the men building defences, destroying petrol stocks and delivering messages, while:

> *There would be important jobs for women, too – not perhaps as dangerous and spectacular jobs as those allocated to the men, but jobs which must be done. They will render first aid to any casualties. They will provide and arrange for food for the defenders... If the telephones are still working, women will be needed to send messages...* Hylton, pp. 95-6

Boys would be recruited as messengers but: 'The place for the girl is in the home, helping her mother with food supplies and bandages, taking care of the little ones and seeing they are kept safe and out of the way.'

Part of the British Isles was in fact occupied; the Channel Islands were overrun by the Germans in July 1940. For various reasons, their experience (documented by Bunting and Cruikshank, among others) was not a valid basis for generalising about what might have happened in England. First, the Channel Islands were demilitarised before their occupation; all the British armed forces were pulled out in recognition of the fact that they were indefensible. Consequently, there was little purpose in resistance on the part of the islands' population and it was actively discouraged by the British Government. In Britain, by contrast, until such time as the country was completely overrun (or even after that, if war continued to be conducted from the outposts of Empire) civilian resistance could have been seen as underpinning the efforts of the Allied armed forces.

Second, Hitler wanted the occupation of the Channel Islands to be a propaganda model of Anglo-German co-operation since (at least at the time of the initial occupation) he still hoped to secure a negotiated peace with Britain. The absence of any real civil disobedience made it easier for the occupying forces to exercise a light control. There was also a disproportionately heavy German presence, relative to the size of the native Islander population – 37,000 troops to a post-invasion population of 60,000 civilians. Again, this would have been a strong disincentive to resistance. Had German troops attempted to occupy Britain as well as those parts of continental Europe they already held, at the same time as conducting a war on other fronts, they would have been very much more thinly spread and a correspondingly more tempting target for guerrilla activity.

In addition, the Channel Islands did not have the complicating factor of the Home Guard. By September 1940, Britain had over 1.6 million men geared up for a form of armed resistance that the Germans regarded as being outside international law. Continental experience suggests that any military success enjoyed by the Home Guard would have been followed by disproportionate reprisals against the civilian population. Whether this would have hardened or deterred any further action by the Home Guard must be a matter for speculation.

Even in the Channel Islands, once their propaganda value was lost, the Germans reneged on a number of the promises they had made to the civilian population, and the Islanders found parts of their population being deported and the remainder living close to starvation.

We know something of the German plans for ruling a defeated Britain from the Gestapo Handbook, published after the war. It was prepared by Walter Schellenberg, a lawyer and SS General and protégé of Reinhard Heydrich, head of the secret police arm of the SS, (the *Sicherheitsdienst*, or SD). It included a list of some 2,820 people, many of them public figures, who were to be arrested or 'taken into protective custody.' The list, compiled 'hurriedly and carelessly' by Schellenberg, included people who had long since ceased to be residents in Britain (either through emigration or death). Professor Franz Six was to have been in charge of rounding up these and other forces of opposition,

The brief Heydrich gave Professor Six was as follows:

> *Your task is to combat, with the requisite means, all anti-German organisations, instructions and opposition groups which can be seized in England, to prevent the removal of all available material and to centralise and safeguard it for future exploitation. I designate London as the location of your headquarters... and I authorise you to set up small Einsatzgruppen in other parts of Great Britain as the situation dictates and necessity arises.*

This cull was likely to have included Boy Scouts ('a disguised instrument of power for British cultural propaganda') active trades-unionists, Communists and Freemasons ('a dangerous weapon in the hands of Britain's plutocrats against National Socialist Germany'), as well as Jews. Six later demonstrated his aptitude and enthusiasm for such a task on the eastern front, where he was responsible for rounding up and executing Soviet political commissars. He received a twenty-year sentence as a war criminal at Nuremberg.

An occupied Britain would have been stripped of both raw materials and

VE Day, and this community is hanging Hitler in effigy, prior to putting him on their bonfire.

manufactured products beyond those needed to maintain the population at a bare subsistence level, and much of the male population would have been deported to Germany and its satellites, to work in the industries there. Von Brauchitsch issued orders which specified that:

> *The able-bodied male population between the ages of seventeen and forty-five will, unless the local situation calls for an exceptional ruling, be interned and despatched to the Continent with the minimum of delay... The welfare of the inhabitants and the interests of the country's national economy...will be considered in so far as they contribute directly or indirectly towards the maintenance of law and order and the securing of the country's labour for the requirements of the German troops and the German war economy...* [The Chief Supply Officer would seize:] *such stocks of food, petrol, motor transport, horse-drawn vehicles, etc. as have not already been taken over by the armies...* [The

following goods would be requisitioned:] *Agricultural products, food and fodder of all kinds, ores, crude metals (including precious metals), cut or uncut precious or semi-precious stones, leather, furs, hides and timber.* [The defeated population would be allowed to keep only those goods] *which are part of a normal household stock.* Orders concerning the organisation and function of military government in England, 9 September 1940

Thus would an occupied Britain have become a slave economy to its conquerors. It would have been divided into six 'Military Economic Commands', with justice meted out by an administrative branch of the army (at least for as long as military operations were still in progress). As in France, the Germans would have relied to some extent upon the existing civilian authorities to run day-to-day services:

> *The English authorities may continue to function if they maintain a correct attitude... Law and order will be established. Administrative measures will not violate international law unless the enemy has given cause for reprisals... When taking hostages those persons should if possible be selected in whom the **active** enemy elements have an interest... Armed insurgents of either sex will be dealt with with the utmost severity.*

By 'utmost severity' they meant the death penalty for possession of firearms or wireless transmitters, or for the posting of seditious notices. With such penalties, and the threat of reprisals against families or neighbours, it must be open to question how many people would have gone down the road of active resistance, or followed Churchill's advice to 'take one with you.'

Kent and Sussex played a central part in one of the most important pivotal moments of twentieth-century world history. In what is perhaps the most comprehensive counter-factual history of the 'invasion' (Macksey, 1980) it takes less than three weeks from the first German landings in Britain to the removal of Churchill and his Government and their replacement with a Vichy-type regime (intriguingly, under the leadership of Major General J F C Fuller, one of the inter-war prophets of the blitzkrieg). The whole subsequent history of the war, and of everything in world history that has flowed from it since, could have been rewritten in those years when Kent and Sussex formed Britain's front line.

Select Bibliography

Angell, Stuart. *The Secret Sussex Resistance* (Middleton Press, 1996)

Ashworth, Chris. *Action Stations 9: Military Airfields of Central South and South-east England* (Patrick Stephens, 1985)

Barnett, Correlli. *The Collapse of British Power* (Eyre Methuen, 1972)

Bethell, Nicholas. *The War Hitler Won* (Allen Lane, 1972)

Boorman, H R P. *Hell's Corner 1940* (*Kent Messenger*, 1942)

Bowyer, Michael J. F. *The Battle of Britain: Fifty Years On* (Patrick Stephens, 1990)

Briggs, Asa. *The BBC: The First Fifty Years* (Oxford UP, 1985)

Brooks, Robin J. *Kent Airfields in the Second World War* (Countryside Books, 1998)

Brooks, Robin J. *Kent Airfields Remembered* (Countryside Books, 1990)

Bunting, Madeline. *The Model Occupation: the Channel Islands under German Rule 1940-45* (Harper Collins, 1995)

Burridge, D. *Twentieth Century Defences in Britain: Kent*

Cantwell, John D. *The Second World War: a Guide to Documents in the Public Record Office* (PRO Handbook No. 15) (PRO, 1998)

Chappell, Mike. *The Canadian Army at War* (Osprey, 1985)

Churchill, Winston S. *The Second World War* (Guild, 1949) (Five volumes)

Cockett, Richard. *Twilight of the Truth; Chamberlain, Appeasement and the Manipulation of the Press* (Weidenfeld and Nicholson, 1989)

Cocks, A E. *Churchill's Secret Army* (The Book Guild, 1992)

Collier, Basil. *The Defence of the United Kingdom* (HMSO, 1957)

Collyer, David. *East Kent at War in Old Photographs* (Sutton, 1994)

Crook, Paul. *Sussex Home Guard* (Middleton Press, 1996)

Cruikshank, Charles. *The German Occupation of the Channel Islands* (Sutton, 1990)

Danchev, Alex and Todman, Daniel (eds). *War Diaries 1939-1945*, Field Marshall Lord Alanbrooke, (Weidenfeld and Nicholson, 2001)

Darwin, Bernard. *War on the Line: the Story of the Southern Railway in Wartime* (Southern Railway, 1946)

Davies, W J K. *The Romney, Hythe and Dymchurch Railway* (David and Charles, 1975)

De Courcey, Anne. *1939: The Last Season* (Thames and Hudson, 1989)

Divine, David. *The Nine Days of Dunkirk* (Faber, 1959)

Doherty, Martin A. *Nazi Wireless Propaganda: Lord Haw-Haw and British Public Opinion in the Second World War* (Edinburgh UP, 2000)

Dover Express and East Kent News

Fleming, Peter. *Operation Sea Lion* (Pan, 1975)

Forty, George. *Tank Warfare in the Second World War* (Constable, 1998)

Glover, Michael. *Invasion Scare 1940* (Leo Cooper, 1999)

Gulvin, K R. *The Kent Home Guard* (North Kent Books, 1980)

Halpenny, Bruce B. *Fight for the Sky* (Patrick Stephens, 1986)

Hastings, Max. *Overlord and the Battle for Normandy 1944* (Michael Joseph, 1984)

Hastings and St Leonards Observer

Hastings and St Leonards Observer 'Hastings and St Leonards in the Front Line' (1945)

Hayward, James. *Myths and Legends of World War Two* (Sutton, 2003)

HMSO. *Roof over Britain. the Official Story of Britain's Anti-aircraft Defences 1939-42* (HMSO, 1943)

HMSO. *Persuading the People: Government publicity in the Second World War* (HMSO, 1995)

Hogg, Ian V. *The Guns 1939-45* (Ballantyne, New York, 1970)

Hopkins, Harry. *The New Look: A Social History of the 1940s and 1950s in Britain* (Secker and Warburg, 1963)

Hough, Richard and Richards, Denis. *The Battle of Britain* (Hodder and Stoughton, 1989)

Humphreys, Roy. *Hellfire Corner: Reminiscences of Wartime in South East England* (Sutton, 1994)

Humphreys, Roy. *RAF Hawkinge in Old Photographs* (Sutton, 1991)

Hylton, Stuart. *Their Darkest Hour* (Sutton, 2001)

Jenkins, Roy. *Churchill* (Macmillan, 2001)

Johnson, J. E. *Full Circle: the Tactics of Air Fighting 1914-1964* (Ballantine, 1964)

Jorgensen, Christer and Mann, Chris. *Strategy and Tactics: Tank Warfare* (Amber Books, 2001)

Kent Aviation Historical Research Society. *Kent Airfields in the Battle of Britain* (Meresborough Books, 1981)

Kent Messenger

Kieser, Egbert. *Operation Sea Lion* (Cassell, 1997)

Kirkham, Josephine (ed). *Rye's War* (Rye Museum Association, 2002)

Knowles, David J. *With Resolve, with Valour* (Knowles, 2002)

Lamb, Richard. *The Drift to War 1922-39* (W. H. Allen, 1989)

Latham, Colin and Stobbs, Anne. *Pioneers of Radar* (Sutton, 1999)

Lawlor, Sheila. Churchill and the Politics of War 1940-41 (Cambridge UP, 1994)

Leslie, Kim and Readman, Alan. *West Sussex at War 1939-1945* (West Sussex County Council, 1995)

Livesey, Anthony (ed). *Are We at War? Letters to* The Times *1939-45* (Times Books, 1989)

Longmate, Norman. *The Real Dad's Army: The Story of the Home Guard* (Hutchinson Library Services, 1974)

Longstaff-Tyrrell, Peter. *Front Line Sussex* (Sutton, 2000)

Longstaff-Tyrrell, Peter. *Barracks to Bunkers: 250 Years of Military Activity in Sussex* (Sutton, 2002)

Lowry, Bernard (ed). *Twentieth Century Defences in Britain* (British Council for Archaeology, 1996)

Lucas, James. *Storming Eagles: German Airborne Forces in World War 2* (Cassell, 1988)

Mackenzie, S. P. *The Home Guard* (Oxford UP), 1995)

Macnab, Geoffrey. J *Arthur Rank and the British Film Industry* (Routledge, 1993)

Macksey, Kenneth (ed). *The Hitler Options: Alternate Decisions of World War II* (Greenhill Books, 1998)

Macksey, Kenneth. *Military Errors of World War Two* (Cassell, 1987)

Macksey, Kenneth. *Invasion: The Invasion of England July 1940* (Collier Macmillan, 1980)

Margach, James. *The Abuse of Power: the War between Downing Street and the Media* (W.H. Allen, 1978)

Minns, Raynes. *Bombers and Mash: The Domestic Front 1939-45* (Virago, 1980)

Montgomery, Bernard Law. *The Memoirs of Field-Marshal the Viscount Montgomery of Alamein,* K G (Collins, 1958)

Murrells, Joseph. *Million Selling Records* (Batsford, 1984)

Ogley, Bob. *Kent at War* (Froglets, 1994)

Parker, Matthew. *The Battle of Britain July-October 1940* (Headline, 2000)

Parker, R A C. *The Second World War* (Oxford UP, 1989)

Ponting, Clive. *1940: Myth and Reality* (Hamish Hamilton, 1990)

Porter, Mary Haskell. *Hastings in Peace and War 1930-45* (Ferndale Press, 2002)

RAF Manston History Club. *RAF Manston in Old Photographs* (Two volumes, Sutton, 1993, 1994)

Reuth, Ralf Georg. *Goebbels* (Constable, 1993)

Robinson, Anthony. *RAF Fighter Squadrons in the Battle of Britain* (Arms and Armour, 1987)

Rootes, Andrew. *Front Line County* (Robert Hale, 1980)

Saunders, Andrew. *The English Heritage Book of Channel Defences* (Batsford, 1997)

Saunders, Andrew. *Fortress Britain* (Beaufort, 1989)

Schactman, Tom. *The Phoney War 1939-40* (Harper and Row, 1982)

Schellenberg, Walter. *Invasion 1940: The Nazi Invasion Plan for Britain* (St Ermin's Press, 2000)

Shaw, Frank and Joan (eds). *We Remember Dunkirk* (Hinckley, Leicestershire, 1990)

Smith, Victor. *Front Line Kent* (Kent County Council, 2001)

Smurthwaite, David. *The Ordnance Survey Complete Guide to the Battlefields of Britain* (Webb and Bower, 1984)

Sussex Express and County Herald. *The War in East Sussex* (1945)

Thornton, David. *Hastings: A Living History* (Hastings Publishing Company, 1987)

Tsouras, Peter G (ed). *Third Reich Victorious: Alternate Decisions of World War Two* (Greenhill, 2002)

Warner, Philip. *The Battle of France 1940* (Cassell, 1990)

Wills, Henry. *Pillboxes: A Study of UK Defences 1940* (Leo Cooper, 1985)

Wright, Patrick. *Tank* (Faber, 2000)

Wybrow, Robert J. *Britain Speaks Out 1937-87: A social history as seen through the Gallup data* (Macmillan, 1989)